Food & Drink

FAMILY CLASSICS

·

Favourite recipes from *Radio Times'* readers

Introduction by Michael Barry
Edited by Alison Field

GW00383042

NETWORK BOOKS

Thanks to: Susie Magasiner, Hattie Ellis, Maria Monk, Becca Allen,
Lizzie Main and Helen Boswell.

Network Books is an imprint of BBC Books,
a division of BBC Enterprises Limited
Woodlands, 80 Wood Lane, London W12 0TT

First published 1994
© in this compilation: Bazal Productions Ltd 1994
© introduction Michael Barry
© recipes: the contributors
ISBN 0 563 37030 0

Set in Bembo by Ace Filmsetting Ltd, Frome, Somerset
Printed and bound in Great Britain by Clays Ltd, St Ives Plc
Cover printed by Clays Ltd, St Ives Plc

Other **Food & Drink** books available from BBC Books:

Michael Barry's **Food & Drink** *Cookbook*
The Big **Food & Drink** *Book*

Other **Radio Times** books available from Network Books:

Radio Times *Around Britain Guide: The Heart of England*
Radio Times *Around Britain Guide: London and the South East*
Radio Times *Around Britain Guide: The North West*
Radio Times *Book of Sporting Dates*
Radio Times *TV & Radio Puzzlebook*
Radio Times *TV & Radio Trivia Quiz Book*

CONTENTS

₤3.65

EDITOR'S NOTE   4

INTRODUCTION   5

TRADITIONAL HOME COOKING   7

THRIFTY FAMILY MEALS   67

RECIPES FROM ABROAD   91

INDEX   127

Beatrice and Bertram Waite (see Lemon Bomb Pudding, page 21).

EDITOR'S NOTE

The quantities used in the recipes in this book have been calculated as accurately as possible. However, because most of them have been handed down, often by word of mouth, the amounts and methods will probably have been adjusted over the years.

The original recipes might have called for 'a handful of sultanas' for example, or 'cook in a large pie plate' depending on the available ingredients and cooking equipment.

Many of them are quite adaptable to suit personal taste so you may prefer to use herbs different to those suggested in the recipe, add a little garlic or use pears instead of apples.

INTRODUCTION

The idea for this book first emerged in Turkey. The setting was a waterside restaurant just along the bay from the city of Marmaris and the occasion a dinner with some newly-met friends on a sailing holiday. As we enjoyed the *meze* and other Turkish specialities, conversation inevitably turned to food and, in this case, what made for family tastes and traditions. It turned out that all of us had recipes that had been handed down through generations, modified slightly for personal tastes, ingredients and health, but with clear lines of descent going back years. 'I've got this marvellous recipe for apple chutney,' was one of the promises, 'I'll send it to you when we get back.' The recipe itself is reproduced overleaf, but it sparked off an idea to run a competition, through **Radio Times** and **Food & Drink**, inviting people to send in their favourite family recipes. The response was immense with people from all over Britain sending in recipes that had been handed down from generation to generation.

The success of the **Radio Times** competition further inspired the idea for **Food & Drink** *Family Classics* which brings together the best of those entries which have become family favourites.

Food is one of the great connectors in human society. What we eat, and the way we eat it, is one of the great delineators of our way of life. An hour in a supermarket or food shop will tell you more about the people you are amongst than any number of learned articles. So too will the recipes we think worth preserving.

In my family there's a very simple way of preparing runner beans when they're at their newest and freshest. The technique came from my grandmother. But even for my children, tasting them buttery and peppery in a big bowl with brown bread and butter, brings back the Welsh valley and the simple farming community that they actually never knew themselves, except through contact like this. The recipes in this book aren't just delicious things to eat or moments of nostalgia. They draw on living skills and ingredients as well as bringing the past, our ancestors and their way of living, back into our kitchens, onto our tables and into our lives.

The other extraordinary thing about this collection is how skilled and ingenious the recipes are, despite their creators' lack of equipment, technology and resources. They often produced dishes that were both elegant and delicious when money or food was scarce, particularly during wartime rationing.

Over the last few years I have done quite a lot of research into the food of earlier times, searching through the archives and ancient manuscript cookery books. Time and again I've been struck by just how much better the dishes can be than any modern equivalent I know. This is partly because the recipes are richer. Before the days of health warnings, butter and cream were lavished in a way that we wouldn't even consider now. But also the skills are often finer, the understanding of the ingredients greater, the balancing of the dish more considered and careful. I hope you will find this the case with the recipes in this book. Here, by the way, is the chutney recipe that set all of this off. It comes from Tricia Llewellyn via her mother-in-law.

SWEET APPLE CHUTNEY

1.2 litres (2 pints) spiced vinegar
900 g (2 lb) small onions, thinly sliced
2.75 kg (6 lb) cooking apples, chopped
900 g (2 lb) sugar
25 g (1 oz) turmeric powder
25–50 g (1–2 oz) cornflour

Put the spiced vinegar in the pan with the onions. Cook for 15 minutes. Add the apples and boil until apples and onion are cooked. Add the sugar and turmeric (just enough to get the right colour) and boil again for 5 minutes. Thicken with the cornflour. Pour into jars and seal.

Michael Barry

TRADITIONAL HOME COOKING

RABBIT STEW 9

MOTHER'S BAKED RABBIT 10

RABBIT COOKED IN MILK 11

JUGGED HARE AND FORCEMEAT BALLS 12

MOTHER MAUD'S
NORFOLK GAME PLATTER 14

NANNA CRAWSHAW'S
NECK OF MUTTON STEW 16

BANANA CHUTNEY 17

PICKLED MARROW 18

CHEESE AND BACON WHIRLS 19

GRANDMA'S SEASON PUDDING 20

———— • ————

LEMON BOMB PUDDING 21

LEMON CREAM AND RATAFIA CAKES 22

GRANDMA'S LEMON TARTS 24

SWISS CREAM 26

CHOCOLATE CREAM 28

GREAT GRANDMOTHER MASON'S
CREAM PUDDING 30

TIPSY PUDDING 33

BET'S BREAD PUD 34

ISLE OF WIGHT PUDDING 35

GRANNY SCOTT'S
WHISKY FLAMBÉ CLOOTIE DUMPLING 36

APPLE STIRRUP 38

SUFFOLK POND PUDDING 39

GRANDMA BENBOW'S
STICKY MARMALADE TART   40

AUNT POLLY'S
CLOVE AND APPLE PUDDING   42

CHOCOLATE BISCUIT CAKE   43

YOUMA LOAF   44

PEPPER CAKE   46

REEVE CAKE   48

SHALEY CAKES   50

OLD ENGLISH CIDER CAKE   51

AUNT LOUISE'S CAKE   52

SPONGE CAKE   53

MILK BREAD   54

EASTER BISCUITS   57

GREAT GRANDMOTHER'S
CHRISTMAS PUDDING   58

MINCEMEAT   60

ALICE'S CHRISTMAS CAKE   62

FOAMING BRANDY SAUCE   64

TOFFEE   65

CHAPEL TOFFEE   66

RABBIT STEW

Janet Hewlett, Exeter, Devon

Clara Wornum was born in Hampstead in 1850. She worked for her father, Alfred Wornum, a piano maker, who had workrooms in Store Street in London's West End. Clara married a Frenchman, Augustus Monopedian, and they had five children. 'Clara used to walk from Hampstead to her father's piano workshop, which must have taken about two hours. I like to think of her returning to a meal of Rabbit Stew with her family after she had climbed up the long hill to Hampstead', says her great-granddaughter, Janet.

Clara's recipes have been enjoyed for three generations, and her Rabbit Stew is a particular favourite with Janet and her family.

SERVES FOUR

50g (2oz) butter
300ml (10fl oz) chicken stock
25g (1oz) flour
1 rabbit, jointed
2 onions, sliced
half a lemon, sliced
1 bay leaf
*salt and freshly ground black
   pepper*
150ml (5fl oz) red wine

Pre-heat the oven to gas mark 4, 180°C (350°F).

Make a gravy with the butter, stock and flour in a flameproof casserole dish. Add the rabbit joints, onion, lemon slices and bay leaf, and season to taste with salt and pepper.

Cover and bake in the pre-heated oven for about 45 minutes.

Add the red wine and cook for 5 more minutes.

Clara Wornum.

9

MOTHER'S BAKED RABBIT

Marjorie Haynes, Weston-super-Mare, Somerset

Rabbit was the most common meat in Sally Peacock's kitchen – beef and chicken were untold luxuries.

She was born in 1878, married George Lucas a farm worker and they had six children. They lived for a time in an old Elizabethan farmhouse near Horsham in West Sussex, where her daughter, Marjorie Haynes, was born.

One of the estate keepers, a bachelor, lodged with them and, in return for mending his clothes, he kept Sally supplied with rabbits. She was a dab hand at skinning and drawing them.

'Mother had six children to feed on a meagre income, but she always managed to provide us with a satisfying meal. I have wonderful memories of her baked rabbit,' Marjorie recalls. 'Jacket potatoes were frequently on the menu in my childhood because the coal-fired kitchen range was permanently alight – along with the bricks wrapped in flannel at bedtime, which were used as bedwarmers . . . How I loved to feel the warmth against my cold feet.'

SERVES EIGHT

2 young rabbits (wild, if possible)
flour, well-seasoned with salt,
freshly ground black pepper
and dried thyme, for coating
25g (1oz) pork dripping or lard
600ml (1 pint) rough cider
300ml (10fl oz) stock
450g (1lb) carrots, sliced
8 baby turnips
450g (1lb) shallots
225g (8oz) streaky bacon
*   or belly pork, cut into bite-*
*   sized pieces*
1 bay leaf
sprig of thyme

Pre-heat the oven to gas mark 3, 160°C (325°F).

Roll the rabbit pieces in the seasoned flour, covering them thoroughly. Quickly brown them in a frying pan in the heated dripping or lard. Place the rabbit in a large casserole or other heatproof dish with a lid.

Add the remaining ingredients to the casserole, cover and bake in the pre-heated oven for 2 hours or until the rabbit is tender. The gravy should be thick enough, but if not, mix a tablespoon of cornflour with a little cold water, add to the casserole and heat, stirring, until it has thickened. Taste and adjust the seasoning if necessary.

Serve with boiled or jacket potatoes and a green vegetable – Marjorie says Savoy cabbage sets the rabbit off particularly well.

10

RABBIT COOKED IN MILK

Rebecca Hilton, Norwich.

Elizabeth Eva Deeley was born into a farming family in Buckingham in 1899. At the age of 23, she married another farmer, Ralph Adams, and they had three children.

Elizabeth Adams.

Farming did not bring in much money and to make ends meet in the 1930s, Elizabeth took in paying guests, for whom she made farmhouse teas on her oil stove. Her daughter, Rebecca Hilton, remembers the sign outside the farm advertising 'TEA WITH HOVIS'.

One dish that cost virtually nothing, thanks to Ralph's skill with a gun, was rabbit, cooked in milk. It was a family favourite and brings back happy childhood memories for Rebecca.

SERVES FOUR

750g (1½lb) rabbit, jointed (about 1 rabbit)
seasoned flour, for coating

50g (2oz) butter
100g (4oz) unsmoked bacon or belly pork, diced
2 large onions, sliced
2 carrots, diced
1 small onion, stuck with 2 cloves, 1 bay leaf and sprig of thyme
1 stick celery, sliced (optional)
1 parsnip, sliced (optional)
salt and freshly ground black pepper
600ml (1 pint) milk
3 tablespoons chopped fresh parsley

Pre-heat the oven to gas mark 4, 180°C (350°F).

Roll the rabbit joints in the seasoned flour and fry gently in the butter until golden. Place them in a casserole dish.

Fry the bacon and onions in the pan you used for the rabbit, then add to the casserole. Add the remaining vegetables to the casserole dish. Season to taste with salt and pepper and pour the milk over. Place the lid on the casserole and cook in the pre-heated oven for 1 hour. Add more milk, if necessary, and cook for another hour.

Add more flour if the gravy needs thickening, check the seasoning and add the parsley. Serve with mashed potatoes and a green vegetable.

11

JUGGED HARE AND FORCEMEAT BALLS

Anita Coon, Cockermouth, Cumbria

Edmund John Ward was born in 1874. He became an architect, surveyor and civil engineer based in the Strand, London. He was very fond of good food and every day would walk down the road as far as Simpson's where he would indulge in a traditional English lunch.

One of his favourite foods was game. Luckily, a perk of his job was an endless supply of hares, pheasants and grouse, given to him by his grateful clients. He would take them down to Eastbourne on the train every weekend for his wife Margaret to cook.

Jugged Hare and forcemeat balls were often on the menu in Eastbourne and John's granddaughter, Anita, remembers her own father, Lewis, skinning and drawing the hare. 'It was always cooked in the same pot, which was large and black. The accompanying vegetables were baked potatoes and sprouts from the garden. Fifteen forcemeat balls were then fried until crisp and brown.'

Ask your butcher to prepare the hare and to cut it into portions. The butcher will also provide you with the carton of blood necessary to make the Jugged Hare.

Right: Edmund John Ward.

1 hare (preferably hung for about
  14 days)
salt and freshly ground black
  pepper
450g (1lb) lean ham, chopped
1 large onion, studded with
  8 cloves
900ml (1½ pints) chicken stock
the saved blood of the hare
350ml (12fl oz) red wine
  (Burgundy, or Rhone wine
  or port)
bouquet garni, including 1 bay
  leaf, parsley, fresh thyme and
  peppercorns

For the Forcemeat Balls
8 tablespoons fine fresh
  breadcrumbs
75g (3oz) margarine
1 tablespoon chopped fresh
  parsley
1 tablespoon chopped fresh thyme
juice and grated rind of ½ a
  lemon
1 egg, beaten
pinch of freshly grated nutmeg
salt and freshly ground black
  pepper

Pre-heat the oven to gas mark 2,
150°C (300°F).

Dry the pieces of hare with kitchen
paper and season with salt and pepper.

Place the hare and ham in a fairly
large flameproof and ovenproof pot
with a tight-fitting lid. Put the onion
in the middle of the pot. Pour over
the stock, blood and wine and add
the bouquet garni. Bring the mixture
almost to the boil, put on the lid and
transfer to the pre-heated oven (or
bottom oven of an Aga) and bake for
3 hours or until the meat is tender.
The temperature will be almost
boiling throughout the cooking pot
which is just as it should be, the meat
will be very tender and the wine and
blood will not curdle.

Make forcemeat balls half an hour
before hare is ready. Combine all the
ingredients, adjust amount of herbs
and salt to taste. Shape into rounds,
about the size of a plum and fry in
hot olive oil until brown all over.
Drain. Keep warm in a gravy boat.

When the hare is ready, Pour some
of the gravy over the forcemeat balls.

Serve with baked potatoes, sprouts
and redcurrant jelly.

Beware of the shot!

MOTHER MAUD'S NORFOLK GAME PLATTER

Jonathan Claxton, Inverurie, Aberdeenshire

At the turn of the century, the large country houses of Norfolk provided vast amounts of game from their estates. Shooting was a popular pastime and, at Sandringham, Edward VII held his famous shooting parties. Then, huge banquets were held where game was served as one of the many courses.

Frederick William Claxton ran a large and thriving family business as a game dealer in Thetford at the end of the nineteenth century. He dealt in large quantities of rabbits, hares and venison and supplied the London markets as well as exporting them to France.

He brought home a lot of spare game for dinner and his wife Maud spent a lot of time concocting different recipes to make use of it all. She was a schoolteacher and, when she married Frederick, he was a widower with a large house and an unruly family.

As a young boy Jonathan Claxton remembers that his grandfather used to reminisce about the wonderful taste of his stepmother Maud's food and the intense aromas of her cooking wafting up the stairs from the dining-room.

Her game platter relies on a variety of game that is braised for a long time over a low heat. The legs of rabbit and hare are often better than the breasts, as the legs tend not to dry out. Jonathan Claxton says that it is the perfect meal for a chilly autumn or wintry night 'when you can pick fresh juniper berries and the game is coming into season. Prepare it in the morning, go for a long walk to get up a good appetite and the platter will be ready to eat when you get back. It is wonderful eaten with a beefy red wine or a tot of single malt!'

SERVES FOUR

jointed pieces of game (pheasant, pigeon, rabbit, hare and venison chops, including the livers, kidneys and hearts, with none of the game having been hung long)
1 carrot, chopped
6 fresh sage leaves, finely chopped
4–5 tablespoons olive oil
salt and freshly ground black pepper
6 fresh juniper berries
50g (2oz) butter
2 onions, chopped
thick slice of smoked bacon, cubed
juice of one orange
a little orange peel
150ml (5fl oz) game stock
croûtons from 3 rounds of bread

Pre-heat the oven to gas mark 2, 150°C (300°F).

*Below: Frederick and Maud Claxton with their family.
Jonathan's father is standing behind Maud.*

Mix the meat with the carrot, sage, olive oil, pepper and juniper berries and then leave to marinate overnight.

Heat enough oil and butter in a flameproof casserole dish to fry the onions, add the marinated meat with the marinade ingredients and seal. Add the bacon, offal, orange juice and a scraping of orange peel. Lightly season with salt, cover, and cook in the pre-heated oven for at least 5 hours. The bottom oven of an Aga is ideal.

Remove the bones and arrange the meat on a large serving platter. Deglaze the pan with the game stock, scraping up the offal and residue, and spoon over the meats.

Decorate with the croûtons. Serve with redcurrant jelly, mashed potato and seasonal vegetables.

NANNA CRAWSHAW'S NECK OF MUTTON STEW

Pauline Wainwright, Loughborough, Leicestershire

Sarah Ellen Evans was born in 1888. Her father Ernest, was a mill worker during the day for a long time, but, after years of studying at night school, he eventually became an author and lecturer in botany and biology at the Burnley Institute.

Sarah married Edwin Crawshaw in 1914 and they lived, with their two children, in Blackpool. Her granddaughter, Pauline Wainwright, remembers her Nanna's simple, tasty cooking from when she was a child: 'She was a typical Lancashire housewife who made a little go a long way. This recipe is special because it is strongly associated with my happy childhood. It was always more than a meal as it was filled with Nanna's love and warmth, too. My father sometimes brought a bottle of Spanish Sauterne for Sunday dinner. Nanna didn't really approve of that. Instead she drank dark brown, somewhat exotic sarsaparilla out of stone jars. These jars would then be used as hot water bottles!'

Pauline with Nanna in 1959.

SERVES FOUR

850g (2 lb) neck of lamb
1½ tablespoons pearl barley
2 tablespoons lentils
2 onions, sliced
3 carrots, diced
salt and freshly ground black
*   pepper*
1 bay leaf
½ teaspoon rosemary or
*   1 teaspoon parsley*
water or *stock to cover*

Put all the ingredients into a large saucepan and cover with water or stock. Bring to the boil and simmer gently for about 2 hours, stirring frequently to prevent it sticking. Top it up with boiling water if the stew becomes too thick.

Serve with mashed potatoes and fresh crusty bread.

BANANA CHUTNEY

Irmgard Dallibar, Ashtead, Surrey

Irmgard Dallibar was born in Prussia. She trained and worked as a nurse and, while on holiday on a boat cruising down the Rhine, she met an Englishman, whom she married, in 1954.

She spoke very little English and could hardly cook at all. Her mother-in-law, Nelly Donovan (born in 1877 in Rye, Sussex), was, however, an excellent cook and a great inventor of dishes. She died just before the birth of Irmgard's first daughter in 1955, but left behind many delicious recipes.

This recipe for Banana Chutney is a well-established favourite with Irmgard, her own daughters and their friends: 'It is always liked by all our visitors from abroad and has been copied many times.'

MAKES ABOUT 1.25 KG (2½ LB)

4½ bananas
225g (8oz) onions
100g (4oz) dates
100g (4oz) raisins
225g (½ lb) brown sugar
½ teaspoon ground ginger
450ml (15fl oz) malt vinegar
2 teaspoons salt
2 teaspoons turmeric

Chop the bananas, onions and dates.

Mix with all the other ingredients and boil until the mixture becomes fairly thick, then simmer, covered, for about 45–60 minutes. If it becomes too thick, add a little more vinegar.

When the chutney is ready, spoon it into warm, sterilized jars and seal straight away. Label the jars when cold.

PICKLED MARROW

Elysteg Edwards, Aberystwyth, Dyfed, Wales

Mary Wigley was born in 1896 on a farm in a small, rural village called Darowen in Montgomeryshire. Welsh was always spoken on the farm. Mary's grand-daughter, Elysteg Edwards, says the name Wigley derives from Dewigley – a French Huguenot name. Her ancestors had fled to Wales to escape persecution from Louis XIV.

'I remember my grandmother loved to make pickles, jams and chutneys and they were all delicious. This is my absolute favourite. My granny had handwritten recipes which are very precious to us all. She died aged 92.'

Mary Wigley.

MAKES THREE TO FOUR JARS

1.75 kg (4 lb) marrow, cubed
salt
1.2 litres (2 pints) vinegar
30 shallots, chopped
450–750 kg (1–1½ lb) sugar
a few cloves
4 chillies
10 g (¼ oz) ground ginger
10 g (¼ oz) mustard powder
20 g (¾ oz) turmeric

Put the marrow cubes into a bowl, sprinkle with salt and leave overnight.

The next day boil the vinegar, shallots, sugar and spices together for 10 minutes.

Add the marrow and boil gently for 40–50 minutes, until the cubes are clear and tender.

Pot the pickle in warm, sterilized jars and seal. Leave for at least a fortnight before eating.

CHEESE AND BACON WHIRLS

Pauline Murphy, Nottingham, Nottinghamshire

This is an old recipe devised by Sarah-Jane Pye who was born near Preston, Lancashire, in 1886. She married Laurence, a local farmer, and they reared their own pig for slaughter and made cheese in the farm dairy. She would make her own flaky pastry and this recipe used up odd bits of cheese from the dairy and bacon from the farm. The bacon whirls would be taken to the men in the fields to sustain them during harvesting.

The recipe has been handed down through four generations to Pauline Murphy, and is always a huge success. These days, of course, they are more likely to be eaten at parties or as nibbles with drinks. Children love them and guests always request the recipe, which Pauline has never revealed – until now!

MAKES TWENTY

250-g (9-oz) packet frozen flaky pastry, defrosted
225 g (8 oz) rindless streaky bacon
50–100 g (2–4 oz) Lancashire cheese, crumbled
1 egg, beaten

Pre-heat the oven to gas mark 7, 220°C (425°F).

Roll out the pastry until it is quite thin, making a square about 25 cm (10 in) each side.

Stretch the streaky bacon using the back of a knife until it is almost transparent.

Lay the bacon strips in vertical lines on the pastry.

Sprinkle the crumbled cheese over the pastry square and roll it up, just like you would a Swiss roll.

Cut it into 20 slices and place them on a dampened baking tray. Brush with the beaten egg, then bake in the pre-heated oven for 20 minutes or until golden brown. Serve warm.

Sarah-Jane Pye.

GRANDMA'S SEASON PUDDING

Sylvia Swain, Heaton, West Yorkshire

Clara Ellen Shepherd, née Potterton, was born in 1878 and was one of 15 children. She, together, with many of her siblings, went to Canada, but Clara didn't settle very well and returned to Yorkshire.

Life was tough for her in the 1920s and 1930s as her husband was often out of work. But she was a good manager of her housekeeping money and she kept her family well fed on inexpensive, filling dishes. One such example that has survived in her family is given here.

'My grandmother was never too exact in the quantities, but it was *always* delicious, even though the pudding was slightly different each time!', writes her granddaughter, Sylvia Swain. 'The recipe was passed down to me and I have scaled down grandma's quantities. In those days, the first course was always Yorkshire pudding and was eaten with the instruction that whoever ate the most pudding would have the most meat!'

Although this is a recipe to eat with roast pork, it is so popular with everyone that one of Sylvia's friend's family demands it whatever roast meat is being served! It is similar to stuffing, but is baked in the oven alongside the joint so that the top is crispy and the underneath is moist. The recipe makes two large puddings—each enough for four to six people.

MAKES TWO LARGE PUDDINGS

450g (1 lb) onions
175g (6 oz) fresh breadcrumbs
225g (8 oz) pork sausagemeat
2 tablespoons chopped fresh sage
salt and freshly ground black pepper
1 small egg, beaten
50g (2 oz) butter

Chop the onions, put them into a saucepan, barely cover them with water and boil until the water has almost all evaporated.

Mix the remaining ingredients, except the butter, together with the onions. Form the mixture into two equal-sized sausage shapes and lay one each side of the roast, placed in a greased roasting tin. Dot the butter on the top of the puddings and bake as required by your roast.

Clara with granddaughter Sylvia, 1940.

LEMON BOMB PUDDING

Garth Waite, Isle of Seil, Argyll, Scotland

Beatrice Whiteside was born in 1882 in the village of Nethercot near Bourton-on-the-Water, Gloucestershire. Her father, Thompson Whiteside, ran the village grocer's shop.

As a young woman, she was taught dressmaking and later worked for Charles Barnett, a wholesale fishmonger in Cheltenham. In 1914, she married Bertram Waite, who had come to live in Cheltenham to work as a representative for a piano dealer. The First World War broke out soon afterwards and Bertram was sent to the Front in France when he joined the Royal Artillery. Luckily, he survived the War and returned home in 1918.

Their son, Garth Waite, now lives on the Isle of Seil in Scotland and remembers his mother being a competent cook and an innovator. He still has a well-thumbed copy of *Mrs Beeton's Book of Household Management*, which was given to Beatrice and Charles as a wedding present.

He recalls that 'her basic suet puddings used the same mixture, producing an amazing variety of first- and second-course meals: we ate steak and kidney pudding, suet dumplings with boiled beef, spotted dick, roly-poly, rhubarb, apple, blackcurrant and gooseberry puddings – most of them boiled in cloths – all derived from the one flour, one breadcrumb, one suet recipe.' The recipe here was usually of a lighter sponge mixture, but it, too, was occasionally clothed in the basic suet mixture.

Garth and his sister are now in their seventies and have enjoyed good health all their lives, despite their early rations of 'heavy, "indigestible" food and unpasteurized milk delivered in open cans to be poured into a jug at the back door . . .'

SERVES FOUR

4 trifle sponges
225g (8oz) golden syrup
120g (4½oz) raisins
75g (3oz) fresh breadcrumbs
100g (4oz) plain flour
2 eggs, beaten
85ml (3fl oz) brandy
1 lemon

Break up the sponges roughly into a bowl and mix in all the other ingredients except the lemon.

Pour the mixture into a buttered heatproof pudding basin or mould, then plunge the whole lemon deep into the mixture. Steam for 2½ hours and serve with a sweet sauce of your choice or custard.

LEMON CREAM AND RATAFIA CAKES

Jennifer Hodgkin, Witham, Essex

This recipe comes from a book entitled *Old Recipes as Used in the Pease and Gurney Households in the XVIII Century*. The Hodgkin family, from Witham, Essex, have been passed these recipes through many generations. One ancestor was Jane Chapman Gurney, who was born in 1757 and died in 1841, and it was from her household that the recipe for Ratafia Cakes came. She was the aunt of the reformer Elizabeth Fry, famous for her work at Newgate Prison.

The Lemon Cream recipe, which tastes like syllabub, was used first by Lydia Richardson, who was born in 1710 in Whitby. She was the grandmother of Edward Pease (1767–1858), who was a well-known industrialist from Darlington and is often called the Father of the Railways. Apparently, George Stephenson wrote to Pease, asking if he might be interested in using a steam railway to transport his goods from Darlington. Edward Pease was something of a philanthropist and agreed, on the condition that the train could carry passengers and, therefore, help the local community. The world's first passenger railway train travelled from Stockton to Darlington, thanks to Edward Pease.

In the old recipe book there are some rather peculiar-looking words such as 'gnipooh Hgouc' and 'slewob stnialpmoc', which must have been

printed so as to preserve Victorian decorum – the words are spelt backwards and usually refer to some medical problem!

The original recipe for the Lemon Cream goes as follows, while the modern version is given below it:

Take a pint of thick Cream grate into it the out rind of two fresh Lemons and squse the Juice into half a Jack of white wine and sweeten it with bet Lofe Sugar take the whites of two eggs well bet, put all into a broad bole and whisk it with a clean whisk for half an Hour then scim of with a Spoun and put in Glasses for use.

SERVES FOUR TO SIX; MAKES EIGHTEEN CAKES

For the Lemon Cream
*600 ml (1 pint) double cream
grated rind of 2 lemons and
175 ml (6 fl oz) juice
25–50 g (1–2 oz) sugar
2 egg whites*

For the Ratafia Cakes
*2 egg whites
175 g (6 oz) caster sugar, sifted
100 g (4 oz) almonds, chopped
½ tablespoon rose water
1 teaspoon flour*

Make the Lemon Cream. Whip the double cream until just short of stiff.

Stir in the lemon rind and juice. Sweeten with the sugar to taste.

Beat the egg whites until they are stiff, then gently fold into the mixture. Spoon into serving glasses and refrigerate overnight.

Now, make the Ratafia Cakes. Pre-heat the oven to gas mark 4, 180°C (350°F). Beat the egg whites until fluffy and combine with the sugar. Mix the almonds with the rose water and flour and add to the egg mixture. It should not be runny, but, rather, firm enough to hold its shape when you spoon it out on to rice paper on a baking sheet or, simply, a greased baking sheet in small balls about the size of a 50p piece. Bake them in the pre-heated oven for 8 minutes or until set. Leave them to cool on a wire rack, then transfer to an air-tight container so they stay crisp until you serve them the next day with the lemon cream.

GRANDMA'S LEMON TARTS

Dorothy Corcoran, Louth, Lincolnshire

Lucy-Anne Brunt was born in 1880 and taught her grand-daughter, Dorothy, how to make this delicious tart on her coal oven. She raised seven children and, despite living in extreme poverty, grandma always provided her family with good, well-balanced meals. She made her own bread every day using 9.5 kg (21 lb) flour a week; the family devoured a sack of potatoes a week, too! Most of the vegetables and fruit came from the garden, but the rest of the groceries were fetched from the grocer's by her children, using a large home-made trolley. Each child was allowed to choose one main meal per week from grandma's 'table d'hote'.

Grandma's Lemon Tarts failed only once: during the Second World War the grocer inadvertently sold her soap powder instead of ground rice. Soapy lemon foam spread all over her precious coal oven!

MAKES FOUR SMALL TARTS OR ONE LARGE

175 g (6 oz) shortcrust or frozen, defrosted pastry
about 25 g (1 oz) butter
100 g (4 oz) caster sugar
1 tablespoon of ground rice
juice and grated rind of 1 lemon
1 egg, beaten

Roll out the pastry until it is about 5 mm (¼ in) thick. Line 4 large, heatproof saucers or one 20-cm (8-in) diameter pie dish. Line with foil and fill with rice or dried peas and bake at gas mark 6, 200°C (400°F) for about 15 minutes or until the pastry is firm and just lightly coloured. Turn the oven temperature down to gas mark 4, 180°C (350°F).

Melt the butter and then stir in the sugar, ground rice and lemon juice and rind. Stir in the beaten egg, then spoon the mixture into the prepared pastry cases or case. Bake in the oven for approximately 20 minutes or until the filling has set.

Serve cold – if the family doesn't get there earlier.

Right: Lucy-Anne Brunt with six of her children, c1917.

SWISS CREAM

Tony Jessop, New Milton, Hampshire

Bessie Mills was born in Blackheath in 1865 and had four children. Her grandson, Tony Jessop, remembers her as a small, round-shouldered lady who always wore a black dress with a lace collar for afternoon tea. 'She always provided home-made jam, scones and cake . . . and, of course, tea, from a silver pot. There was the added excitement of the tiger-skin rug, complete with stuffed head, on the drawing-room floor – a trophy brought back from India by my uncle.'

Bessie was a keen cook and this was one of her favourite recipes, which has been handed down to Toby. He now cooks it for *his* grandchildren, who love it.

SERVES FOUR

2 tablespoons plain flour
600 ml (1 pint) milk
juice of 3 lemons and peeled rind
of 1 lemon
50 g (2 oz) caster sugar
4 crystallized lemon slices
4 tablespoons whipped cream
4 sugary biscuits

Mix the flour with a little of the milk to form a smooth paste.

Pour the rest of the milk into the top of a double saucepan together with the lemon rind. Heat it slowly

Bessie and her granddaughter,
Tony's sister Anne, 1926.

and, most important, do not boil. Then, remove the rind, bring the milk just to boiling point, and, straight away, pour it on to the flour mixture, stirring. Pour the mixture into a saucepan together with the sugar. Heat it and stir constantly until it is thick. Boil it for 8 minutes, stirring, then turn it into a large bowl and leave it to cool, stirring occasionally.

When it is almost cold, stir in the lemon juice.

Serve, cold, in individual bowls, topped with a crystallized lemon slice and a spoonful of whipped cream, together with a sugary biscuit (Tony Jessop remembers that his grandmother used to serve Playmate biscuits, which were available before the War – they had faces on them and were very popular with children in those days.)

CHOCOLATE CREAM

Betty Skelton, Redhill, Surrey

Sophie Jumeau came from the Loire Valley where her grandparents worked the land. Her own parents were tailors and, in the 1870s, they moved to Paris. Sophie inherited their tailoring skills and became a dressmaker – eventually she worked for the great fashion houses of Paquin and Worth.

Sophie married a peripatetic English tailor called Will Shepherd in 1898 and the first years of their marriage were spent constantly on the move. One daughter, Marie, was born in Dublin, another in Liverpool and a third in London! A fourth child was expected when the family was *en route* for Germany, but Sophie, tired of the nomadic life, refused to go any further than Paris, where a son was born in 1906. They finally settled near Versailles, west of Paris.

Marie was sent to her father's family in Birmingham at the age of 14 to perfect her English. She returned to France to continue her education, but that all ended at the outbreak of the First World War. The family lived near a major railway depot where ambulance trains ferried the wounded and sick soldiers from the Front. Marie's ability to act as interpreter was greatly appreciated, and she met a lot of British soldiers, including Albert Hughes, whom she invited home whenever he had a few hours leave.

She became a war bride when they married in January 1918.

Sophie and Marie were both busy women who cooked quick, simple meals and liked to improvise. 'Money was usually tight when I was a child and everything that wasn't finished up at one meal would re-appear "en salade", "en croquettes" or in a soup,' recalls Betty, Marie's daughter. 'She never ate desserts but provided them for her five children, and, when she could spare the milk and eggs, made Chocolate Cream – this was always a lovely surprise and a treat.'

You can vary the flavour by substituting part of the milk with coffee essence or a liqueur.

SERVES SIX

600 ml (1 pint) milk
4 eggs, at room temperature
40g (1½ oz) sugar
35g (1¼oz) cocoa powder
few drops vanilla essence

Pre-heat the oven to gas mark 2, 150°C (300°F).

Warm the milk slightly.

In a bowl, beats the eggs lightly then mix in the sugar.

Sift the cocoa powder if necessary and mix it into the eggs and sugar. Add the vanilla essence.

Add the warm milk and mix well,

Below: Sophie with her daughters Marie and Dorothy.

making sure all the sugar has dissolved. Pour it into an ovenproof dish or 6 individual ramekins and place in a roasting tin, pouring in enough cold water to come 1 cm (½ in) up the sides. Cook in the centre of the oven for 1 to 1½ hours, until it has set.

Serve cold, decorated with whipped cream.

GREAT GRANDMOTHER MASON'S CREAM PUDDING

Janet Brown, Cookham, Berkshire

In 1911, Fanny Mason began to write an account of her life, beginning with the words: 'Strangers meeting me in my sixty-ninth year would little guess that the stout old granny had once been the heroine of a real-life romance, or the central figure of many stirring incidents.'

Fanny's father died when she was eight and, two years later, her mother was persuaded that Fanny would be better off at a clergy orphan school in St John's Wood, but conditions were tough: 'At breakfast and tea, no plates, but a hunk of bread about two inches thick with a scraping of butter on it, moistened with milk and water served from large urns. A repast of this served at 6pm was called supper. For dinner we had a helping of beef or mutton and two potatoes. I do not remember any pudding but rice. On Saturdays, we had a mysterious stew. On Good Friday, we had two buns, but no bread for breakfast, boiled rice with pepper and salt for dinner and one bun for supper. Truly we did fast.'

A cholera epidemic broke out in the school and, because her own house was cold and damp, Fanny's widowed mother reluctantly agreed that it would be better for Fanny to go and live with her Aunt Jenefred, who had offered to complete her education and provide for her. Jenefred had a violent temper and made Fanny's life a misery. Once, Jenefred broke her arm and Fanny wrote: 'During the six weeks of Aunt's helplessness I had more peace than during the whole ten years of my stay with her. My persecution began again when she recovered . . . one service she rendered me, I was taught how to do everything connected with a house, including cooking.'

Fanny fell in love at 17 with James Mason, but her mother begged him to put her out of his mind because she knew Aunt Jenefred would disapprove of this young man of no means. Fanny was distraught and became engaged to a persistent suitor on the rebound. Fortunately, she was dissuaded from marriage, but recalls that, had it not been for her younger brother – to whom she felt responsible – she would have 'done something desperate – run away and tried to earn my own living'.

James married someone else, but she died in childbirth and so, later, he and Fanny renewed their romance and decided to marry. Such was Aunt Jenefred's hold over the family that the young couple still asked for her consent, which was refused. Nevertheless, they married in 1866 at the Church of St Mary the Less in Lambeth and afterwards spent a glorious fortnight in Paris on their honeymoon.

Below: Fanny Mason and a page from her recipe book.

James and Fanny lived in Princes (now Cleaver) Square in Lambeth. In the winter, James went to work holding two baked potatoes to keep his hands warm. He would give these to the crossing sweeper outside his office who was, it's said, grateful for the free meal. Indeed, Fanny wrote, 'It was in this parish that I came face to face with London poverty.' She and James decided to start a weekly dinner for the poor children of the neighbourhood. 'Having a room built on the garden, we let them come there, the only qualification being poverty and hunger. We made out 20 tickets on which was written "A dinner for a child" and the address. My dear husband took these with him and gave them to any poor little waifs that he saw. I had a boiler that held 3 gallons, and this was enough to supply good soup for 20 children, who were also given a thick slice of bread.'

Fanny and James had a total of nine children, but only four of them survived. She stopped writing her journal in the end because her son said no one would be interested. Her great-granddaughter, Janet Brown, laments that 'none of her descendants have yet forgiven him!' At least her name lives on in this recipe, which is so simple, but tastes quite delicious –

especially with fresh fruit. You can use any alcoholic drink you like to flavour the cream, but, if you are decorating the pudding with fruit, try framboise kirsch with raspberries, Grand Marnier or Cointreau with sliced oranges or another liqueur with its original fruit.

SERVES SIX

8 trifle sponges
300 ml (½ pint) whipping cream
sugar, to taste
sherry or *alternative, to taste*

To decorate
300 ml (½ pint) whipping cream
(optional)
fruit or *fruit purée*

Line a 850-g (2-lb) pudding basin with the trifle sponges.

Whip the cream, sweeten it to taste and flavour it with the sherry or your chosen alternative to taste. Pour the mixture into the lined basin and cover with the remaining trifle sponges. Weight it down by fitting a saucer inside the rim of the bowl and putting a couple of tins on top and chill in the refrigerator overnight.

Cover the pudding with whipped cream and fruit or with fruit purée.

TIPSY PUDDING

Sally Sanford, Mudeford, Dorset

Violet Bessie Etheridge was born and brought up in Eastbourne at the turn of the century. When she left school, she went to work as a telephonist at a local post office where she met her husband. During the Second World War she and her son were evacuated to Hitchin in Hertfordshire, leaving her husband behind – still working at the same post office.

She was a keen tennis player and enjoyed cooking. Her granddaughter, Sally Sanford, remembers many an afternoon spent in her kitchen. 'My grandma judged all the weights by eye and used to say to me that so long as the result was delicious the exact weights didn't matter!'

SERVES SIX

100g (4oz) butter, softened
100g (4oz) caster sugar
2 large eggs, beaten
1 tablespoon coffee essence
3 generous tablespoons good-
  quality dry sherry
8 trifle sponges

Cream the softened butter and sugar together, then slowly beat in the eggs. Beat in the coffee essence and sherry.

Grease a 1.2-litre (2-pint) terrine, slice the trifle sponges lengthwise, then layer them with the creamed mix in the prepared dish. Make sure that you press the layers down fairly well, but you do not need to weight it. Chill in the refrigerator overnight.

Carefully unmould the pudding the next day and decorate with, say, whipped cream if you wish.

Violet with her husband and son, 1943.

33

BET'S BREAD PUD

Flora Shimell, Torpoint, Cornwall

A unt Nell passed down this recipe to Flora Shimell who has turned it into quite a money-spinner. 'Every Saturday in our little Cornish seaside village, we have a coffee morning in the village hall to raise money for various charities. It's also a chance for us "oldies" to meet and have a gossip. I make two Bread Puds, which are taken out of the oven at 10am and, by 10.30am, I will have arrived at the coffee morning with each cut into 36 pieces . . . 15 minutes later, they are all sold out. Fairy cakes, sponges, tarts – they are all left standing by my Bread Pud! Visitors to the village ask for some to take home and pay a small sum to charity for the recipe. I used to be a cook in a small hotel, and how I wish I had a shilling for every time I was asked to cook it.'

Nell Hopkins was cook to a branch of the Rothschild family who lived in Eaton Square, London until 1925, when they moved to Leighton Buzzard. Nell moved with them and married the local postman. They lived happily in her little cottage until she died aged 90. Her sisters also baked Bet's Bread Pud and died aged 97 and 103 respectively. It must hold the secret to a long life.

The Bread Puds are most appreciated by Flora's grandchildren when they come home starving from the beach.

SERVES SIX TO EIGHT

850g (2 lb) breadcrumbs
600 ml (1 pint) milk
100g (4 oz) soft brown sugar
350g (12 oz) any mixed dried fruit
100g (4 oz) peel
50g (2 oz) self-raising flour,
  sifted
3 teaspoons mixed spice
225g (8 oz) margarine, melted
2 tablespoons golden syrup
1 tablespoon marmalade
2 large or 3 small eggs, beaten
2 tablespoons demerara sugar
1 teaspoon ground cinnamon

Soak the breadcrumbs in the milk overnight. Next day, pre-heat the oven to gas mark 4, 180°C (350°F). Break up any lumps and put the mixture into a large bowl. Mix in the sugar, dried fruit, peel, flour and mixed spice. Add the margarine, golden syrup, marmalade and eggs and mix well.

Grease a loaf tin approximately 28 by 33 cm (11 by 13 in) and transfer the mixture to it, pressing it down and flattening the top. Bake for about 1 hour, but after 30 minutes, take it out of the oven and sprinkle the demerara sugar, mixed with the cinnamon, over the top and return to the oven for the remaining time.

Serve hot or cold, cut into slices.

ISLE OF WIGHT PUDDING

Suzanne Whitewood, Newport, Isle of Wight

Frances Lambert was such a marvellous cook that she was banned from entering local cooking competitions because she would otherwise *always* carry away all the top prizes!

She was born in London at the close of the nineteenth century and, on leaving school, trained first as a milliner and a dressmaker. Then moved to Worthing where she trained as a cook.

In the 1920s she and her husband set up a small guesthouse on the Isle of Wight. Later, they moved to a bigger hotel and, in 1930, it was one of the few establishments in Ventnor to boast hot and cold running water in each of its ten bedrooms!

When war broke out, Frances transferred her cooking and organizational skills to the local Services canteen, where she became a second 'mother' to many visiting servicemen.

Frances' granddaughter, Suzanne Whitewood, remembers growing up with an atmosphere of home cooking: 'I often used to help granny fill jam tarts and make butter cream for her sponge cakes . . . She created the recipe for Isle of Wight Pudding as a celebration of the Island's fresh, home-produced ingredients, which seemed much better than those in her native London. Grandad grew the fruit on his allotment, which also supplied the hotel with vegetables.'

SERVES SIX

100g (4oz) butter or lard
225g (8oz) flour (preferably half wholemeal, half white self-raising flour)
120ml (4fl oz) honey
225g (8oz) fruit (blackcurrants, raspberries)
120ml (4fl oz) single cream

Pre-heat the oven to gas mark 6, 200°C (400°F).

Rub the butter or lard into the flour until the mixture resembles breadcrumbs. Mix to a stiff pastry dough with about 1 tablespoon cold water.

Roll the pastry out to about a 5-mm (¼-in) thickness and so it is a rectangular shape.

Spread the honey over the pastry and scatter the fruit evenly on this. Roll it up, roly-poly pudding fashion, and place in a greased ovenproof pie dish. Pour the cream over and bake in the pre-heated oven for 45 minutes to an hour or until the pastry has turned a lovely golden brown.

GRANNY SCOTT'S WHISKY FLAMBÉ CLOOTIE DUMPLING

Mazda Munn, Dalry, Ayrshire, Scotland

The Clootie Dumpling is an old Scottish tradition. One dumpling can feed a multitude, so they were invaluable in the days when there were many mouths to feed, and each family probably has their own version, handed down through generations.

Lizzie McLay was born the third child of eight in Paisley in 1891. She married John Scott in 1913 and they had six children, who, in turn, gave her nine grandchildren. One of these granddaughters, Mazda Munn, remembers Granny Scott's big family parties, particularly on Bonfire Night, Christmas Eve and Hogmanay: 'Her famous Clootie Dumpling was always prepared and was just the thing for cold Scottish nights! It goes particularly well with mulled wine.' Granny Scott used to add to the children's excitement by putting silver sixpenny bits or a single half crown (wrapped in greaseproof paper) into the Clootie Dumpling.

Mazda has often cooked dumplings outdoors on an open fire as 'this adds a sense of excitement to the dish!' She says it can serve up to 30 people as it's very filling.

An essential piece of equipment needed for preparing this recipe is a 'cloot', which is a white cotton cloth approximately 76 cm (30 in) square. A pillowcase or a piece of sheeting will do fine.

SERVES UP TO THIRTY

750g (1½lb) self-raising flour
  (preferably wholemeal)
½ teaspoon ground nutmeg
2 teaspoons ground mixed spice
2 teaspoons ground ginger
2 teaspoons ground cinnamon
40g (1½oz) porridge oats
400g (14oz) soft brown sugar
225g (8oz) vegetable suet
225g (8oz) raisins
225g (8oz) sultanas
50g (2oz) crystallized ginger
1 carrot, grated
1 apple, grated
1 tablespoon black treacle, melted
  into a little milk
silver trinkets individually
  wrapped in greaseproof paper
  (optional)
white flour, for dusting

For the flambé
50g (2oz) demerara sugar
175ml (6fl oz) of whisky, rum
  or Drambuie

Mix all the ingredients, except the trinkets and white flour, in a very large bowl until the mixture is of a dropping consistency, but not too runny. Add the trinkets now if you wish to include them.

Sterilize the cloot by boiling it for 10 minutes.

Lizzie and John Scott.

on a flat surface and sprinkle flour evenly over it while it is still hot. Place the cloot, floured side uppermost, over a colander and spoon in the dumpling mixture.

Tie up the cloot firmly, leaving room for the dumpling to expand, but not leaving any openings in the cloth. Slap the dumpling for luck, then lower it into the boiling water and cover the pan. Keep it on the boil for 4–4½ hours, topping up with more boiling water when necessary.

When the dumpling is firm, remove it from the saucepan and unwrap it carefully. Try not to damage the 'skin' that will have formed. Lift it gently from the cloot to a large ovenproof plate. Sprinkle with the demerara sugar, pour the whisky, rum or Drambuie over the dumpling, turn out the lights, flambé and serve.

Alternatively, omit the flambé and put the dumpling into a pre-heated gas mark 7, 220°C (425°F) oven for 20 minutes to firm up.

Either way, it goes well with cream or chestnut sauce.

Half fill a large saucepan with water and place a small heatproof plate or a saucer in the bottom (to prevent the dumpling from sticking to the bottom of the pan). Bring the water to the boil.

Place the sterilized cloot in the boiling water for a few minutes. Remove it from the water and wring it out, but keep it as hot as possible (wear rubber gloves). Spread the cloot

APPLE STIRRUP

Janet Towill, Cirencester, Gloucestershire

Daisy Scott was born in 1882 and spent most of her life in Dorchester. She married a carpenter and lived a traditional country life. Her granddaughter, Janet, spent most of her summer holidays with Daisy and learnt to cook in her kitchen. 'She gave me the enthusiasm to experiment with recipes and be more adventurous.'

Daisy's recipe for Apple Stirrup, meaning 'stir up', was probably the result of her own inventiveness. Janet says it tastes a bit like a traditional Dorset apple cake, but has a softer, pudding style. She still enjoys making it regularly because it's very economical and it remains a great family favourite especially for Sunday lunch.

SERVES FOUR

100g (4oz) self-raising flour
40g (1½oz) brown sugar
scant tablespoon suet
pinch of ground cinnamon
150ml (5fl oz) milk
4 large apples, sliced

Pre-heat the oven to gas mark 4, 180°C (350°F).

Mix all the ingredients, leaving the apples until last. There needs to be more apple pieces than mixture, which should be fairly sloppy.

Spoon into a greased pie dish and bake in the pre-heated oven for about 30 minutes or until it has turned golden brown. Serve with butter and brown sugar to taste.

Daisy Scott in 1913.

SUFFOLK POND PUDDING

Margaret Moreton, Newport, Gwent, Wales

Tom Smith was born and bred in Suffolk and did not leave the county until he joined the Merchant Navy in the 1920s. For a few years, until the Second World War, he was a pastry chef on the P&O liners, travelling to and from the Antipodes.

He always used to return to England with booty bought abroad and enjoyed rather a reputation as a 'big spender', according to his nephew, Rex Moreton. Rex's wife, Margaret, was taught how to make Suffolk Pond Pudding by Tom. She remembers Tom recalling how mystified the passengers were when 'Suffolk Pond Pudding' appeared on the ship's menu. 'What mystified me was how the galley managed to produce all the individual ones he said were served in the dining-room. When I serve it to my guests, they speculate how like a Suffolk pond it is – firm edges and dark mysterious depths.'

Mix the flour and suet together and bind with a little cold water. Work all the ingredients into a ball. Roll out to about a 5-mm (¼-in) thickness.

Mix the sugar, sultanas, currants, peel and butter together in a bowl.

Line a greased, heatproof 600–900 ml (1–1½-pint) pudding bowl with the rolled out dough, leaving enough to form a lid. Pour in the fruit mixture and seal with a lid of the remaining dough. Fasten a circle of greased greaseproof paper and a pudding cloth (or else use a basin with a clip-on lid) over the basin, tying it firmly down under the rim with string, and boil for 4 hours.

SERVES FOUR

150g (5oz) self-raising flour
50g (2oz) suet
50g (2oz) brown sugar
(muscovado if you have it)
50g (2oz) sultanas
50g (2oz) currants
pinch of cut peel
25g (1oz) butter

Tom Smith.

GRANDMA BENBOW'S STICKY MARMALADE TART

Anne Boldry, Tiverton, Devon

Gertrude Benbow was born in Bridgnorth, Shropshire, in 1883. She began her working life as a kitchen maid in a large country house and, by the age of 23, had worked her way up to become the cook. Her day started very early: she had to prepare the breakfast – kidneys, kedgeree, fresh rolls, the works – and finished late after preparing large formal dinners.

Life was not all work and no play, though, because Gertrude found romance. She fell in love with the head gardener, William Massey, and, as the age of thirty, married him. However, she is still remembered by her maiden name as Grandma Benbow.

Her Sticky Marmalade Tart is a favourite with her granddaughter, Anne Boldry, who now cooks the tart for her family and friends. 'This recipe is so unique because it uses everyday ingredients to make a special treat. For real luxury, add 2 tablespoons of thin cream and a tablespoon of whisky instead of milk. Serve it with clotted cream – delicious!'

SERVES SIX TO EIGHT

For the shortcrust pastry
275g (10oz) plain flour
pinch of salt
50g (2oz) butter

50g (2oz) lard
3 tablespoons iced water

For the filling
75g (3oz) butter
75g (3oz) caster sugar
2 eggs
½ × 450-g (1-lb) jar homemade marmalade
25g (1oz) flour
3 tablespoons milk

First, make the pastry. Mix the flour and salt together in a mixing bowl. Rub the butter and lard into the flour until the mixture resembles breadcrumbs, then stir in just enough cold water until the mixture comes together. Let the pastry rest in the refrigerator for at least 30 minutes before rolling it out. Pre-heat the oven to gas mark 5, 190°C (375°F).

Line a 23-cm (9-in) tart tin with the pastry and bake blind in the pre-heated oven for 10 minutes until the pastry is just done. Leave the oven on.

Now, make the filling. Cream the butter and sugar until fluffy. Beat in the eggs and then the marmalade. Stir in the flour and the milk.

Pour the mixture into the pastry case, decorate with any remaining pastry scraps, then bake for about 30 minutes or until the filling is set and brown. Serve it warm with custard or cream.

Gertrude Benbow.

AUNT POLLY'S
CLOVE AND APPLE PUDDING

Ann Cottingham, Elham, Kent

Polly Barnes, born in 1902, was famous for this clove-flavoured sponge pudding of hers, made with the apples grown in her Sussex garden. She even topped the pudding with almonds from her own tree. 'Polly was always cooking – making sponges, chutneys and jams and always looking for new ways to cook apples. There was always a wonderful aroma coming from her kitchen,' recalls her niece, Ann. 'I can remember trying to prise whole almonds from their shells using a vice as a nutcracker. Polly would also use plum kernels in jams to give them a bit of extra bite.'

Aunt Polly used to vary the fruit she used in this pudding, using pears and gooseberries at times. 'It's a very special recipe because it is down to earth, but has the appearance and aroma of a more exotic dish – and it's so easy,' says Ann.

SERVES FOUR

100g (4oz) margarine
100g (4oz) caster sugar
2 eggs, beaten
100g (4oz) wholemeal flour
1 teaspoon ground cloves
450g (1lb) cooking apples,
* cooked and drained (sugar*
* added to taste)*
150g (5oz) sultanas

For the glacé icing
100g (4oz) icing sugar
few drops vanilla essence
* (optional)*
1 tablespoon warm water

Pre-heat the oven to gas mark 4, 180°C (350°F).

Cream the margarine and sugar together until soft. Beat in the eggs, then fold in the flour and ground cloves.

Put three-quarters of the mixture into a greased and floured 25-cm (10-in) loose-bottomed cake tin and cook in the pre-heated oven for 10 minutes.

Remove the cake tin from the oven and spread the apple and sultanas over the mixture. Add the remaining sponge mixture in dollops over the apples and cook for 20 more minutes.

Leave the pudding to cool and, when it is, make the glacé icing. Sift the icing sugar into a bowl and add the vanilla essence, if using. Gradually stir in the warm water, then beat to remove any lumps that may have formed. The icing should be thick enough to coat the back of a spoon, so adjust the consistency – more water if too thick or more icing sugar if too thin – if necessary. Dribble the icing over the pudding straight away and leave for a few minutes to set.

Serve the pudding with cream.

CHOCOLATE BISCUIT CAKE

Louise Boreham, Burntisland, Fife, Scotland

Margaret Wilson went to look after her six-month-old niece, Louise just before the Second World War broke out. Louise's mother had died in 1939. Margaret had been a career woman, so it must have been rather a shock to find herself having to cope in a top-floor tenement flat, with just a Victorian range for heating the kitchen, the water and the cooking, and with a very small child to look after.

Louise can remember her fear when the 'monster' oven was lit as it would frequently 'blow back' causing a small explosion: 'I used to hide until the flame was safely established,' she says. On top of the oven were two gas rings, used for most of the cooking (and for boiling the white washing every Monday), and a kettle and a pot would be kept on a stand on top of the coal fire – Margaret used to perform a juggling act with the pots when she was cooking but she managed to create delicious meals for the family and Louise still uses her hand-written cookery book today. One particular favourite is Chocolate Biscuit Cake. Margaret used broken biscuits which were bought cheaply from a nearby factory. 'The best ones were extracted for the biscuit barrel but the chocolate cake was my preferred treat,' recalls Louise. She was thrilled when Margaret became her step-mother.

Louise has a useful tip for recipes like this one that call for crushed biscuits. To prevent the crumbs going everywhere, put the biscuits in a polythene bag and hold the open end closed while crushing them with a rolling pin.

MAKES SIXTEEN SQUARES

100g (4oz) margarine
1 generous tablespoon golden syrup
2 tablespoons cocoa powder
50g (2oz) raisins
300g (11oz) biscuits (rich tea, digestive or any broken ones), roughly crushed

Melt the margarine and syrup in a saucepan over gentle heat, then add the cocoa powder and stir until a smooth mixture results. Stir in the raisins and crushed biscuits.

Pour the mixture into a greased 20-cm (8-in) square cake tin and leave it to cool. Then, cut it into 5-cm (2-in) squares and store in the refrigerator.

YOUMA LOAF

Fiona Marsden, Liverpool

Agnes Stephenson was born in 1871 and grew up in Liverpool. She was a very strong-willed woman who stood for no nonsense. When she married she was quite adamant that two children were sufficient. She told her husband, William, that on no account would she be a childbearing machine and would not budge from this view. This was quite a feat in the days before birth control. Everyone around her had difficulty in stopping at eight, nine or ten children.

Agnes helped the local doctor when he needed a nurse and would often lay people out in their homes after they had died. The money she earned from this she saved, amassing enough money to buy a piano for her elder son, also called William. Young William later taught his own daughter, Fiona, to play and sing a repertoire of Victorian and Edwardian songs, which she performed at parties.

Fiona Marsden remembers the weekly visits from her grandmother, who would come armed with a cake – fruit, caraway seed or coconut – and recipes to help her mother during the lean War years. 'I particularly remember the mock almond paste, using semolina and almond essence, which was quite wonderful during the War. And, of course, this recipe for Youma Loaf, which has been baked in the family for over 50 years – it's so quick and easy to make.'

MAKES ONE SMALL LOAF

1 egg, beaten
150 ml (5 fl oz) milk
450 g (1 lb) self-raising flour
225 g (8 oz) demerara sugar
150 g (5 oz) sultanas
1 tablespoon treacle or golden
   syrup

Pre-heat the oven to gas mark 4, 180°C (350°F). Grease a 1.2-litre (2-pint) loaf tin.

Pour the egg into a mixing bowl and stir in the milk.

Add all the remaining ingredients together, stirring them well. The mixture should have a soft consistency.

Turn the mixture into the prepared loaf tin and bake in the pre-heated oven for about 1 hour, covering it with foil for the last 15 minutes. It is done when a skewer inserted into the middle comes out clean. Remove the loaf from its tin and leave to cool on a wire rack.

Serve sliced and buttered.

Right: Agnes with sons Leonard and William in 1913.

PEPPER CAKE

Maisie Gray, Prestwich, Manchester

Granny Lawson was born Martha Jane Foster in 1852 and had a tragic childhood. Both her elder sister, Margaret, and her younger brother, William, died in infancy and, when she was two, her mother also died.

Martha was then sent to live with her Aunt Sarah – one of her father's six sisters. Around the same time, another of Martha's aunts, Elizabeth, married George Lawson, a young farmer who had rented a farm at Sherburn about 12 miles inland from Filey in North Yorkshire. They had a son called John. About 18 years later, George died and John carried on managing the farm.

In 1870, at 19, Martha Jane married her 21-year-old cousin, John Lawson. They had four sons and seven daughters and they lived on the farm until John's death in 1917.

The Pepper Cake recipe comes from a book of recipes written by Granny Lawson, but it was most probably handed down to her from her grandmother. Her daughter-in-law, Maisie Gray, remembers making it, with Martha by her side giving instructions: 'She had no idea of oven temperature as the kitchen range had no thermostat. Nevertheless, the cake turned out well and, when it was cooling, my mother said "it takes me back, every Michaelmas we used to make it and we made a cake each for all the married members of the family".' Indeed, all Maisie's family have fond memories of the cake. Maisie likes it spread with butter and a slice of Wensleydale cheese.

MAKES ONE LOAF

450g (1 lb) plain flour
2 teaspoons ground ginger
1 teaspoon ground cloves
2 teaspoons ground coriander
2 teaspoons ground caraway
1 teaspoon bicarbonate of soda
350g (12 oz) black treacle
50g (2 oz) margarine
50g (2 oz) brown sugar
25g (1 oz) candied peel
25–50g (1–2 oz) sultanas (optional)
150 ml (5 fl oz) light ale

Pre-heat the oven to gas mark 3, 160°C (325°F). Grease and line an 18 by 13-cm (7 by 5-in) loaf tin with greased greaseproof paper.

Sift the dry ingredients into a mixing bowl. Warm the treacle and margarine, and add the sugar and fruit.

Gradually add the dry ingredients and mix until well combined.

Add the ale until the consistency becomes soft, then pour the mixture into the prepared loaf tin. Bake for about 1 hour. It is ready when it is firm and has a dark crust.

Below: Martha Jane Lawson.

REEVE CAKE

Stephanie Nestor, Maidenhead, Berkshire

May Reeve was born in 1892 in Hertford – one of 12 children. She had a lovely singing voice, but her parents were nevertheless horrified when May announced that she planned a career as a professional soprano. 'My great-grandparents were simple, country folk and "the stage" was not considered a suitable profession for an innocent young woman!,' says May's granddaughter, Stephanie. However, fate intervened when May went to stay with her sister in London and won a competition to have her voice professionally trained. 'My great-grandmother still forbade her to go to London for the lessons, but May's father managed to get the prize transferred to a singing teacher in Waltham Cross, on the under-standing that one of Nan's brothers would take and collect her in the pony and trap. Great-grandmother would only listen to her in church.'

May married just at the beginning of the First World War, but her happiness was short-lived. Her husband was killed on his return to the Front in August 1917, shortly after attending the christening of their only daughter. 'Nan never remarried and brought up my mother in a tiny cottage with no bathroom, as well as nursing my great-grandmother, who was wheelchair-bound for over 20 years.'

May Reeve.

May continued singing as a hobby and sang with the Co-operative Societies' Choir on BBC Radio in 1926. She was always winning prizes – so much so that when she won a competition for the third year running, the judge, one Sir James

Barker, changed the rules. Rather than award her the same prize (a pair of candlesticks) again, he said he would like to give her a personal gift from his Manor – on one condition: she would have to be able to sing 'Eileen O'Lana', which had been his wife's favourite when she was alive. May's reply was, 'If the pianist can play it, I can sing it!' Sir James was delighted and sent his footman home to get the prize – a clock from his library!

May was a great cook: 'even now I can remember her pastry,' recalls Stephanie. She made dandelion wine, which used to smell like seaweed when it was being brewed.

It was during the Second World War that May invented Reeve Cake, when eggs were hard to come by. Her granddaughter still makes it regularly. 'It's a moist dark chocolate cake, which improves with keeping if not eaten straight away. Not too rich with a wonderfully smooth texture.'

SERVES EIGHT

75g (3oz) margarine
1 tablespoon golden syrup
150ml (5fl oz) water
1 teaspoon bicarbonate of soda
225g (8oz) self-raising flour
25g (1oz) cocoa powder
100g (4oz) granulated sugar
a little icing sugar, for dusting

For the butter cream icing
40g (1½oz) butter, softened
75g (3oz) icing sugar
few drops vanilla essence
½–1 tablespoon milk or warm water

Pre-heat the oven to gas mark 5, 190°C (375°F). Grease a small 450-g (1-lb) loaf tin.

Place the margarine, golden syrup and water in a saucepan and melt them together over a gentle heat. Remove the pan from the heat and add the bicarbonate of soda.

Sift the flour and cocoa together into a mixing bowl and add sugar, then beat in the syrup mixture.

Transfer the mixture to the loaf tin and bake in the pre-heated oven on the middle shelf for about 40 minutes (it may need longer, check after 40 minutes). When the cake is ready, the top will crack slightly. Leave it to cool a little in the tin, then turn it out to finish cooling on a wire rack.

Meanwhile, make the butter cream icing. Cream the butter until it is soft. Sift the icing sugar, then gradually beat it into the butter. Beat in the vanilla essence, then the milk or water, a little at a time until it is the desired thick but soft consistency.

When the cake is completely cool, slice it in half and fill it with the icing. Dust the top with icing sugar.

SHALEY CAKES AND OLD ENGLISH CIDER CAKE

Bunny Parker, Weston-super-Mare, Avon

Edith Lott was born about 1840. When she grew up, she became what was called a 'herb wife', which was a sort of untrained doctor. She did a lot of 'birthing and deathing' as she was so much cheaper than a doctor! She was held to be a wise old woman who knew a lot about herbs and spices.

Edith had very little money, but had been to a Dame School and learned her 'three R's' – reading, 'riting and 'rithmetic. She kept her household accounts up to date and knew where the last penny went.

Her granddaughter, Bunny, remembers going as a child to her house in Brixton: 'She lived in one big room with a bed in the middle. I clearly remember the lovely smell of spices in her room . . . she had bags scattered around filled with cedar wood shavings or camphor wood or even thyme.'

Bunny particularly remembers going to visit Edith in the 1920s: 'We used to love her Shaley Cakes. She always made her own dough, of course, but I use frozen pastry as it's so much easier!'

The other recipe Edith made that Bunny still enjoys today is that for Old English Cider Cake. This cake is delicious and will keep for a long time. It has a distinct flavour and is excellent for picnics.

SHALEY CAKES

MAKES EIGHT CAKES

For the pastry
100g (4oz) flour
1 tablespoon baking powder
pinch of salt
100g (4oz) butter (or *margarine if really necessary*)
75g (3oz) cornflour
25g (1oz) caster sugar
1 egg yolk
100ml (3½fl oz) milk or *water*

For the filling
100g (4oz) lard
3 tablespoons granulated sugar
1 teaspoon mixed spice
130g (5oz) currants and sultanas (preferably soaked for 2 hours or so in hot tea)

Pre-heat the oven to gas mark 6, 200°C (400°F). Grease a 23 × 15-cm (9 × 6-in) baking tin.

First, make the pastry. Put the flour, baking powder and salt into a mixing bowl. Rub in the butter or margarine, then add the cornflour and mix well.

Stir in the sugar (though remember to leave this ingredient out if you want to make savoury cakes to serve with meat pies!).

Beat the egg yolk with a little of

the milk and stir into the centre of the flour mound. Add a little more of the milk as necessary to make a firmish dough.

Turn the dough out on to a floured surface, roll out to a roughly rectangular shape, and add the 'filling' in the following way. Put dabs of lard, each about the size of a walnut, on the rolled-out dough, about 4 cm (1½ in) apart and use about a third of the lard. Sprinkle liberally with the sugar, mixed spice, currants and sultanas. Fold a third of the dough in from each end and then do the same for each side. Turn the package round a quarter turn to the right and roll out again. Repeat this folding and larding twice more.

Roll the dough out until it is the size and shape of the prepared baking tin, score across with a knife to form 8 cakes. Bake in the pre-heated oven for 20 minutes.

OLD ENGLISH CIDER CAKE

SERVES EIGHT

100g (4oz) butter
100g (4oz) sugar
2 eggs, well beaten
225g (8oz) flour, sifted
1 tablespoon bicarbonate of soda
½ nutmeg, grated
200ml (7fl oz) cider

Pre-heat the oven to gas mark 4, 180°C (350°F). Grease a 23-cm (9-in) tin.

Beat the butter and sugar together to form a cream.

Add the eggs, mix them in, then half the flour, sifted in with the bicarbonate of soda and the nutmeg.

Beat the cider in a bowl until it is as frothy as it can be, then pour the butter, egg and flour mix into it. Stir in the remaining flour and mix well.

Spoon the mixture into the prepared tin and bake in the preheated oven for 45 minutes.

AUNT LOUISE'S CAKE

Greta Harries, Hampton Hill, Middlesex

This could, instead, be called the 'Lost and Found Cake'.

Greta Harries' family on her father's side came originally from Ireland, near the Mountains of Mourne. Greta remembers her father recalling a wonderful cake from his childhood, made by his Aunt Louise before she emigrated to New Zealand.

'In 1953 we moved to Middlesex and made friends with our neighbours, a New Zealand family, who were in Britain for a short stay. One day they offered me a piece of delicious cake, which they called Aunt Louise Cake. Could this be the same wonderful cake remembered by my father? Incredibly, it was. In New Zealand there is an old custom of exchanging cakes on baking days with neighbours and Aunt Louise's baking skills had travelled from Ireland to New Zealand, then around that country and had now found their way back to Britain! We were overjoyed as the recipe had been lost to our family. It has now been made many times for relatives and passed on to friends in Canada and the USA – it is a well-travelled cake.'

SERVES EIGHT

120g (4½oz) butter or
   margarine
50g (2oz) granulated sugar

3 large eggs, separated
1 teaspoon milk
few drops of almond essence
225g (8oz) self-raising flour,
   sifted
350g (12oz), approximately,
   apricot or pineapple jam
100g (4oz) caster sugar
100g (4oz) desiccated coconut

Pre-heat the oven to gas mark 5, 190°C (375°F). Grease and lightly flour a Swiss roll tin.

Cream the butter or margarine and granulated sugar well until you have a smooth mixture. Add the egg yolks, the milk and the almond essence.

Add the sifted flour gradually and fold it in until it is well mixed in.

Place spoonfuls of the mixture on to the prepared Swiss roll tin. With floured fingers, spread the mixture over the surface of the tin. Spread the jam over the mixture.

Whisk the whites of the eggs until stiff. Gently fold the caster sugar into the egg whites with a metal spoon, then fold in the desiccated coconut.

Spread the coconut topping evenly over the jam and bake for about 30 minutes, until it is just golden (be careful not to burn it).

Leave it to cool on a wire rack, then cut it into squares. They can be served with a lemon sauce if desired and keep well.

SPONGE CAKE

Edna Noble, Otley, West Yorkshire

This simple sponge cake has been enjoyed for more than 250 years by six generations. Octogenarian Edna Noble, from West Yorkshire, remembers how her mother won prizes with it at various shows. Her crowning glory was a prize at the Royal Show when it was held at Harrogate.

'She baked her cakes in an old-fashioned side oven, fired by wood and coal,' Edna remembers. 'This cake was baked in a copper tin shaped like an old-fashioned beehive, that is perfectly round and coming down in rounded tiers. The cake was 7½ in deep and light beyond belief.' The tin was greased with melted lard and then some caster sugar was spooned in and shaken around it until the inside was covered with sugar. 'The cake was a picture when it was baked, with the outside crust glazed and golden,' says Edna. Edna bitterly regrets giving away the beehive tin, but still enjoys the cake and has passed the recipe on to her daughter.

SERVES EIGHT TO TEN

350 (12 oz) caster sugar
5 large eggs
150 ml (5 fl oz) water
250 g (9 oz) plain white flour,
  sifted

Pre-heat the oven to gas mark 4, 180°C (350°F). Grease one or two cake tins and coat with caster sugar, tipping out the excess sugar.

Whisk the eggs until they are light and fluffy.

Put the water and the remaining sugar in a saucepan and bring to the boil. When the sugar has melted, pour the syrup in a thin stream into the egg mixture, beating all the time to combine the ingredients and continue beating until the mixture is cool.

Slowly add the flour, stirring in a figure of eight and lifting the mixture to incorporate air so the finished cake is light.

Pour the cake batter into the prepared tin or tins and bake in the pre-heated oven for about 1 hour, until the cake bounces back when lightly pressed in the middle or a skewer inserted in the centre comes out clean.

MILK BREAD

Rachel Rutter, Nantwich, Cheshire

A century ago, most farmers ran mixed farms and their wives' cooking was based on what was available from the farm business. They reared their own pigs, grew the wheat for bread and kept cows, and there was always plenty of milk and eggs.

Rachel Rutter comes from a long line of Cheshire farmers and, as a child, she remembers thinking that her grandad was French because he had such a broad Cheshire accent!

'Granny always made her own bread, but never wrote the recipe down – she relied on the feel of the dough to get it right.' Rachel has tried to copy the recipe as accurately as she can, but suggests that it can be changed a bit to suit. For example, you can use half white and half wholemeal flour instead of the strong white bread flour given in the ingredients for the basic dough if you like, but you will need to add more liquid.

MAKES ONE LARGE LOAF
OR TWELVE ROLLS

Basic dough
15g (½oz) fresh yeast
  (substitutes just aren't the
  same)
1 teaspoon caster sugar
300ml (10fl oz) milk
50g (2oz) lard

500g (1lb) strong white bread
  flour
1 teaspoon salt

For savoury bread
100g (4oz) cheese, sliced

For sweet or Hot Cross Buns
175g (6oz) currants
50g (2oz) sugar
50g (2oz) butter, melted
1 egg
½ teaspoon mixed spice

Using the back of a teaspoon, cream the yeast with the sugar in a cup. It will go liquid and frothy.

Gently heat the milk together with the lard until it feels warm to your finger. Stir the creamed yeast into the milk mixture and leave until there is a head of froth on the liquid.

Place the flour and salt in a large, warm bowl. (Either use the oven or a microwave on low power to warm the flour through and make the yeast start working more quickly.) Pour in the frothy liquid and work it into the flour with a fork. If you are making sweet or hot cross buns, add the currants, sugar, melted butter, egg and spices at this point.

Turn the dough out on to a lightly floured surface and knead for 10 minutes until it is smooth and elastic. It should feel warm, springy and

Below: Granny Mapes with her children Walter and Mary, c1932.

smooth. If the dough feels at all dry or crumbly, add a little more liquid as dry dough will not rise properly.

Place the dough in a greased bowl in a warm place (near a boiler is perfect), covered with a greased polythene bag (or damp cloth), and let the bread prove until it comes to the top of the bowl (about 1–1½ hours).

Pre-heat the oven to gas mark 6, 200°C (400°F). Grease a 450-g (1-lb) loaf tin or a baking sheet.

Turn the proved dough out on to a board and knock out all the air by kneading it lightly. Shape it into one large loaf, or plait it, and place the dough in the prepared loaf tin or baking tray. Leave it to prove in a warm place until it comes to the top of the tin. Alternatively, divide the dough into 12 pieces, shape into rolls and prove on the prepared baking sheet in a warm place for 20 minutes.

For hot cross buns, simply cut crosses into the tops of the rolls.

If making savoury bread, however, knock the dough back as before, but divide it into three equal portions. Roll out each piece into a long sausage, join the three pieces at one end and plait them over slices of cheese, pressing the ends together when you have reached the ends of the sausages of dough. When it has proved again and is baked, the finished bread has a strand of cheese running through it.

Bake in the pre-heated oven until well risen and golden, about 10–15 minutes for rolls, 20–30 minutes for a large loaf. The loaf or rolls will also sound hollow when tapped on the bottom when they are done. Turn on to a wire rack to cool. (A sticky sugar syrup could be brushed on to hot cross buns hot from the oven to add to their enjoyment!)

EASTER BISCUITS

Violet Collins, Hemel Hempstead, Hertfordshire

Emily Bray was born around 1855 and was a cook to a West Country family who lived in the house that inspired the story of *Little Lord Fauntleroy*. She married a cooper who worked for a local soft drinks factory and they had four boys. The youngest of the brothers was named Reginald and Emily taught him how to cook.

Emily Bray and Reginald, 1890.

These Easter Biscuits were always a favourite each year. The original recipe called for oil of cassia, which comes from cassia bark. This used to be available from chemist shops, but is now very difficult to find. Violet, her gradnddaughter, recommends cinnamon as a good substitute, but she says that it has a milder flavour.

MAKES ABOUT FORTY BISCUITS

275g (10oz) butter
550g (1¼lb) flour
275g (10oz) caster sugar
50g (2oz) currants
2 teaspoons cinnamon
2 eggs, beaten

Pre-heat the oven to gas mark 4, 180°C (350°F).

Rub the butter into the flour.

Stir in the sugar, currants and cinnamon.

Add the eggs and mix to form a stiff dough.

Turn the dough out on to a floured surface and roll out to about a 5-mm (¼-in) thickness. Using a biscuit cutter, cut out the biscuits, re-rolling the dough as necessary until you use it all up. Place them on greased baking sheets and cook them in the pre-heated oven for just about 10 minutes, until they are lightly golden brown.

57

GREAT GRANDMOTHER'S CHRISTMAS PUDDING

Anne-Marie Murphy, Chertsey, Surrey

Henriette Hellman was born in Cologne in 1849. She was a cook for an aristocratic household with kitchens so big that there was even a special room where game was hung to mature.

Henriette first made this pudding in 1876 when she came over from Germany to marry an Englishman. It has appeared on her family's table every Christmas since, for four generations.

During the War, the pudding's ingredients were adapted to suit rationing, with carrots used to sweeten it instead of precious sugar. Dried fruit rations were hoarded for months to get enough for the pudding. One year, the family were waiting in anticipation till it was time to make the pudding. The fruit had been carefully washed and put in front of the fire to dry, but 'The cat found it and ate the lot! My mother and I looked in dismay as the cat vomited up our precious fruit,' recalls Anne-Marie Murphy, Henriette's great-granddaughter – 'It nearly ruined our Christmas!'

On a more gastronomic note, Anne-Marie says, 'Christmas pudding can be very black and dry, but this combination of ingredients makes a moist, delicious pudding with a unique flavour that has earned compliments for over 100 years.'

**MAKES TWO
2.25-KG (5-LB) PUDDINGS**

350g (12oz) self-raising flour
*450g (1lb) large raisins
(preferably Valencia)*
450g (1lb) sultanas
450g (1lb) currants
*100g (4oz) blanched almonds,
chopped*
450g (1lb) moist demerara sugar
350g (12oz) suet
*550g (1¼lb) fresh fine white
breadcrumbs*
225g (8oz) mixed peel
1 teaspoon salt
1 teaspoon mixed spice
1 teaspoon cinnamon
*juice and finely grated rind of
3 lemons*
*juice and finely grated rind of
2 oranges*
3 eggs
*600-ml (1-pint) can good-
quality brown ale*

Sift the flour into a large mixing bowl. Mix all the dry ingredients together and stir well.

Add the juice and grated rind of the lemons and oranges, eggs and, lastly, the ale. The mixture should neither be too wet nor too dry.

Divide the mixture between two greased basins. Tie up with pudding cloths and secure well, then boil for

Henriette Hellman.

8 hours or steam for 10 hours, checking the water level regularly and topping up as necessary. Remove the wrappings and replace them with fresh ones and store the puddings in a cool, dark place for at least a month before eating. Then, boil for 1 hour before serving.

MINCEMEAT

Mary Barnsley, Hagley, Worcestershire

Mary Rees was born in South Wales in 1887 and trained as a professional cook at Cardiff Cookery School. After graduating, she went to London and taught cookery at the Northern Polytechnic School.

Mary Shepherd.

Meanwhile, she continued her romance with a young curate whom she had first met as a student in Cardiff. In 1912, she married Arthur Shepherd in her home town of Pontardawe.

As the wife of a young curate, she had to move house several times. Eventually, Arthur became the Archdeacon of Dudley and then Canon and Vice-Dean of Worcester Cathedral.

This recipe for mincemeat was one of Mary's favourites. Her daughter, who is also called Mary, always makes this mincemeat at Christmas: 'It's particularly tasty – and is much nicer than mincemeat using suet. It is very popular with family and friends, who always ask for the recipe.'

Mary also recommends using dried apricots instead of chopped peel as it makes the mincemeat lovely and moist. Also you can adjust the quantities of nuts or spices according to your tastes.

MAKES ABOUT 3 KG (7 LB)

450g (1 lb) cooking apples, peeled and cored
450g (1 lb) raisins
450g (1 lb) sultanas
450g (1 lb) currants
175g (6 oz) chopped peel or dried apricots
100g (4 oz) ground almonds
100g (4 oz) almonds, chopped (can be fairly coarsely chopped)
½ teaspoon mixed spice, ginger or cinnamon
pinch of salt
350g (12 oz) soft brown sugar
225g (8 oz) butter
100ml (3½ fl oz) sherry, brandy or rum
juice and grated rind of 1 lemon
juice and grated rind of 1 orange

Mary and Arthur's wedding in April 1912.

Put the first six ingredients through a mincer using either a coarse or fine disc (a little brandy can be added at this stage if liked).

Mix the minced and remaining ingredients, except the butter and sherry, brandy or rum, all together and leave, covered, overnight.

The next day, melt the butter and strain it. Then stir it well into the mincemeat, together with the sherry, brandy or rum. Then transfer the mixture to jars and pour a little brandy on top before closing tightly with the lids.

ALICE'S CHRISTMAS CAKE

Laura Wood, Llandysul, Dyfed, Wales

Alice Hill was born in the 1880s near Woking. She never married, but helped to look after her sister-in-law Caroline's five children. Great Aunt Alice would call round every morning without fail to clean and black the stove for Laura Wood's grandma before going on to her job as a maid in one of the large houses nearby. She was adored by all her nieces and nephews because she had great wit, warmth and a sense of fun.

Laura Wood was only three months old when her Great Aunt Alice died in a rather dramatic and tragic way: 'She was killed on her beloved bicycle outside our house on a foggy day. She hadn't heard the car due to increasing deafness. I had just had a bath and my mother, hearing the commotion outside, ran outside with me in her arms. I was stark naked and caught pneumonia and, for a while, it was touch and go as to whether I would survive.

'We eat Alice's Christmas Cake every year – a happy reminder of my Great Aunt.'

MAKES ONE APPROXIMATELY 2.5-KG (5½-LB) CAKE

For the cake
175g (6oz) butter or *margarine*
175g (6oz) caster sugar
3 eggs

50ml (2fl oz) milk
225g (8oz) self-raising flour, sifted
100g (4oz) cherries
225g (8oz) sultanas
½ teaspoon burnt sugar or *treacle (optional)*
100g (4oz) currants
100g (4oz) raisins, chopped
100g (4oz) mixed peel
25g (1oz) ground almonds
½ teaspoon nutmeg
½ teaspoon allspice

For the almond paste
225g (8oz) caster sugar
225g (8oz) ground almonds
1 egg

For the icing
225g (8oz) icing sugar
1 egg white
1 teaspoon lemon juice

Pre-heat the oven to gas mark 2, 150°C (300°F). Grease and line a 20-cm (8-in) baking tin with greased greaseproof paper.

Cream the butter or margarine and sugar together.

Work in the eggs and milk, then, gradually, the flour, followed by the other ingredients. Beat well together.

Transfer the mixture to the prepared baking tin and bake in the pre-heated oven for 4–4½ hours.

Alice Hill (top row, left) with her family.

Leave it to cool on a wire rack.

Meanwhile, make the almond paste. Mix the sugar, ground almonds and egg together until well combined and of a stiff dough-like consistency. Roll the almond paste out on a sugared board to the shape of the cake. Only put it on to the cake, though, when it is quite cold.

Finally, make the icing. Mix the sugar, egg white and lemon juice well together. Spread on top of the almond paste using a knife (keep dipping the knife in hot water to ensure that the icing spreads easily). Decorate the top of the cake with cherries, angelica or anything you like!

FOAMING BRANDY SAUCE

Rosemary Eveleigh, Blackburn, Lancashire

A different accompaniment to the Christmas pudding is Foaming Brandy Sauce. The recipe was handed down to Rosemary Eveleigh from her grandmother, Sarah Stranix. 'This is a well guarded family secret – my sister will probably kill me when she finds out I have sent it to you – but there is just no contest between this and the usual, sickly brandy butters. It's so light, but deliciously alcoholic!'

Sarah's father was the butler to a landed family who had a large estate near Crumlin. When Sarah married Samuel Stranix, she moved to Belfast and, although money was short, she always behaved like a lady: 'My grandmother would never carry the shopping, she always had it delivered.'

Sarah and Samuel had eight children, after which, Sarah decided, at around the age of 45, to take to her bed and hold court from there. She did not want any of her children to marry and, should one of them 'cross' her, she would feign 'a turn' and clutch her heart so that the doctor would be sent for – in this way, she kept them all in line. However, four of them did escape and marry, while four toed the line and stayed with their mother.

Sarah's granddaughter, Rosemary, remembers her sitting at the head of the Christmas dinner table 'like a queen . . . while my mother and aunts slaved in the kitchen. Every year she would say "This is the last Christmas I'll see" and everyone would chorus "of course it's not" and, indeed, it wasn't.' She died at the ripe old age of 96.

MAKES ABOUT 300 ML (½ PINT)

200 ml (7 fl oz) hot water
50 g (2 oz) sugar
100 g (4 oz) butter
2 eggs, separated
1 tablespoon plain flour
brandy to taste

Put the water, sugar and butter into a saucepan. Bring the mixture to the boil slowly, cook for a few minutes then take the pan off the heat.

Beat the egg yolks and flour together, then add to the saucepan and bring to the boil again, cooking for a few minutes (be careful that it does not curdle). (The mixture can be left at the back of the cooker to keep warm at this stage as it needs to be served as soon as the egg whites and brandy have been added.)

Whisk the egg whites until they are stiff.

Take the saucepan off the heat and gently mix in the whites. Add brandy to taste (a good measure, though) and serve in a warmed jug.

TOFFEE

Gillian Drake, Chichester, Sussex

Mrs Lilian Pim included her recipe for toffee in a recipe book she had printed to raise funds for The Victoria Hospital in Woking where she ran the Linen Guild in the early part of the century. The Guild comprised a group of ladies who took charge of repairing all the hospital linen – mostly by hand.

The book's cover illustration was designed by an old schoolfriend of Lilian's and her granddaughter,

Gill Drake, recalls that the original wooden block used to hang over the fireplace in her nursery.

Lilian had so many recipes in her book that she dedicated each to a family member . . . the toffee was dedicated to her grandson.

MAKES ABOUT THIRTY SQUARES

175g (6oz) butter
450g (1lb) granulated or *caster sugar*
65ml (2½fl oz) water
2 tablespoons golden syrup

Melt the butter in a heavy-bottomed saucepan.

Add the sugar, water and golden syrup and stir over a medium heat so it is bubbling with a metal spoon until the mixture becomes thick and brown. To test if it is done, drop a small quantity into a cup of cold water. If it becomes crisp, it is ready.

Spread the mixture over the bottom of a greased shallow 18-cm (7-in) baking tin (or one lined with silicone paper) and mark out bite-size squares with a sharp knife. Leave it to set.

When set, crack the toffee into the marked pieces and, if liked, wrap each piece in a square of greaseproof paper and twist the ends to make up a box of toffees.

Lilian with granddaughter Gillian.

CHAPEL TOFFEE

Rachel Goddard, Thurmaston, Leicestershire

Rachel Goddard remembers being somewhat deprived of sweets as a child growing up in the 1940s – rationing meant there were no such indulgences. However, her father, John, did manage one special treat and that was his Chapel Toffee, so named because he made it while her mother was out on Sunday evenings, at chapel. 'She would return home to find her rations severely depleted. Entirely disregarding my mother's standards of hygiene, Dad always used an old brass preserving pan – not unacquainted with verdigris. The pan would be perched precariously on the enamelled bar of the grate, which contained a coal fire; my mother would have been horrified to know that the fireguard had been removed to cook our toffee! Sometimes, while the mixture was cooling, my brother and I would roll a portion in the palms of our grubby little hands and drop the glistening balls into a bowl of cold water where they hardened like magic. This recipe never fails to remind me of those far-off Sunday winter evenings and the excitement we had making it.'

Rachel and her father John, 1950.

MAKES ABOUT TEN SQUARES

150g (5oz) sugar
40g (1½oz) butter
1 heaped tablespoon golden syrup
large pinch of salt
dash of vinegar

Grease a large, strong pan and put all the ingredients into it. Bring the mixture to the boil slowly, stirring all the time, and then allow it to boil rapidly for about 3–4 minutes until the mixture turns golden brown.

Remove from the heat and pour into a well-greased roasting tin. Cut the mixture into squares before it hardens. When it has, turn the tin upside down and bang hard to remove the toffee, which will be hard and crunchy, like butterscotch.

THRIFTY FAMILY MEALS

POTATO SOUP AND DUMPLINGS 68

WHAT'S INTILLIT SOUP 69

LENTIL SOUP 70

CURRIED LENTIL SOUP 72

AUNT NETTIE'S STEAK LOAF 73

AUNT WINNIE'S BEEF ROLL 74

SAUSAGE STOVIES 76

SCOTCH SCALLOPS 77

BATE PIE 78

TATTIE BAKE 80

MUM'S IMPOSSIBLE PIE 82

THRIFT PIE 83

HERRING AND APPLE PIE 84

AUNTIE'S STEAMED SALMON SOUFFLE 86

FALSE FISH 88

MOCK GOOSE 90

POTATO SOUP AND DUMPLINGS

Olive Stout, Woodford Green, Essex

'Coming home from school in the thirties, cold and hungry, to a bowl of my mother's special potato soup was always a treat,' remembers Olive Stout.

Her mother, Frances Sharland, was born in 1893 in Stourbridge, in the Midlands. She married Thomas Hill who worked as a finisher for Stuart Crystal.

Although the family had very little money, they ate well – even during the Second World War. Thomas grew lots of vegetables and they kept their own chickens, which supplied them with eggs.

Olive still cooks this soup several times each winter to provide a filling and hearty meal.

SERVES FOUR

750g (1½lb) potatoes, peeled
2 medium-sized carrots, scraped
if necessary
1 leek
1 celery stick
2 medium onions
200g (7oz) collar bacon
15g (½oz) margarine
1 beef stock cube mixed into 1.2
litres hot water
a little chopped fresh parsley
salt and freshly ground black
pepper
1 egg, beaten
pinch of nutmeg
50g (2oz) cornflour, plus extra
for dredging

Boil 450g (1lb) of the potatoes until tender. Cut the remainder into 1-cm (½-in) dice. Slice the carrots, leek, celery and onions. Remove the rind from the bacon and chop the meat.

Melt the margarine in a large saucepan, fry the bacon for 1 minute, then add the vegetables. Cook over a low heat for 5 minutes.

Add the beef stock, diced potatoes, parsley and season to taste with salt and pepper. Bring to the boil, cover and simmer for about 20 minutes.

Meanwhile, make the dumplings. Sieve the 450g (1lb) cooked potatoes into a bowl. Add the egg, salt and pepper to taste, nutmeg and the 50g (2oz) of cornflour – mix together well. Turn on to a board and lightly dredge with cornflour. Form into a roll and divide into 8 even-sized slices. Shape each into a round dumpling.

Pour water into a large saucepan until it is two thirds full. Add a pinch of salt and heat. Blend 1 teaspoon of cornflour with a little cold water and add to the saucepan. Bring to the boil, stirring, then add the dumplings. Lower the heat and simmer gently for 10–15 minutes.

Serve the soup with the dumplings on top.

WHAT'S INTILLIT SOUP

Caroline Grey, Bideford, Devon

This recipe was invented by Philadelphia Grey about 50 years ago. Her unusual name is apparently not uncommon in the Shetlands, according to Philadelphia's grand-daughter, Caroline. She says that the trend started when local sailors came home from a voyage to the American city of the same name.

Philadelphia, aged 17.

As for the soup, it was christened when people eating it would ask Philadelphia what was in it. 'My grandmother would say "There's neeps intillit and lentils intillit." "But what's intillit?" would come the reply. "Well, I'm telling you what's intillit – there's neeps intillit and peas intillit." "But what's intillit?", and so on and so on!', remembers Caroline. In the Shetlands, 'What's intillit?' is, in fact, a common expression. Hence the name of this soup. A neep, of course, is a turnip.

This recipe is great for keeping out the cold, and is a real 'throw in' job – made with whatever is to hand.

SERVES SIX

900 ml (1½ pints) marrowbone stock, skimmed
1 onion, chopped
175 g (6 oz) green or yellow or mixed lentils
2 turnips, peeled and diced
1 swede, peeled and diced
50 g (2 oz) dried peas
100 g (4 oz) split barley
3 large carrots, sliced
1 large potato
2 bay leaves
salt and freshly ground black pepper
2 tablespoons chopped fresh parsley

Bring the stock to the boil, add the remaining ingredients, except the parsley, and season to taste with salt and pepper. Boil for 10 minutes, then lower the heat and simmer for a further hour or so (you may need to add another 600 ml/1 pint water or stock during cooking).

Add the chopped parsley and adjust the seasoning if necessary. Serve with crusty bread.

69

LENTIL SOUP

Polly Ridler, Hyde, Cheshire

Patterson Proud was playing as a professional footballer for Sheffield Wednesday when he met and married Sarah McNight in 1909. She had been a housemaid and cook to a family of schoolteachers in County Durham where she became relatively well educated for a girl of her background.

Patterson retired from football and went to work down the local pit. They had two children. Sarah was a keen cook and kept a book of her favourite recipes, including this one.

Her granddaughter, Polly, still likes to cook Sarah's lentil soup: 'My family love it – especially for a good, satisfying winter lunch.'

SERVES SIX

350g (12oz) red lentils
2 onions
3 carrots
1 small swede
2 medium potatoes
50g (2oz) butter
1.75–2.25 litres (3–4 pints)
  stock from boiling bacon or
  water
salt and freshly ground black
  pepper

Leave the lentils to soak for 2–3 hours, then drain.

Grate all the vegetables (this is essential as it determines the texture). Sauté the vegetables in the butter until they are just soft and golden – not browned. Add the stock or water, together with the lentils and simmer gently until the lentils are thoroughly cooked and have virtually disintegrated (about ½ hour). Season with salt and pepper.

Either eat straight away or, better, leave to cool then refrigerate to eat the following day when the flavours have blended and developed.

Right: Sarah Proud.

CURRIED LENTIL SOUP

Mabyn Fletcher, Blandford Forum, Dorset

Annie Drew was born in Helston, Cornwall, in 1849. When she was 21, she married Robert Pickering, a Cheshire farmer. Seven years later, when Annie was pregnant with their fifth child, Robert died.

Robert had a brother, John, who felt it was his duty to take on the responsibility of his brother's young widow and five children and decided that he would like to marry Annie. However, in those days, this was not legal in Britain and so they had to go to France, where they were married in Neufchâtel.

After the wedding, they returned to Chester where they ran a school. Annie taught music and French.

Her granddaughter is now 82. 'I well remember my grandmother and her lentil soup. She handed the recipe on to me. It is most warming and satisfying. Economical and easy to make, it also freezes well.'

SERVES THREE TO FOUR

250g (9oz) red lentils
1 carrot, chopped,
1 onion, chopped
2 celery sticks, chopped
450ml (15fl oz) milk
1 teaspoon salt
freshly ground black pepper
scant ½ teaspoon curry powder
(preferably Madras)
1 teaspoon sugar
25g (1oz) butter

Simmer the lentils in 1 litre (1¾ pints) of unsalted water for 1 hour. Add the carrot, onion and celery and simmer until they are tender (about 30 minutes), stirring from time to time.

Mix together the milk, salt, pepper, curry powder, sugar and butter. Stir the mixture into the lentils and vegetables, stirring gently until the soup thickens.

Left: Annie and John Pickering.

AUNT NETTIE'S STEAK LOAF

Rosemary Randall, East Moseley, Surrey

Janet Milloy – also known as Aunt Nettie – was born in Glasgow 93 years ago and still lives in Scotland. Her Steak Loaf is regularly enjoyed by her niece Rosemary: 'This recipe is in the tradition of a little of something good shared among many. Using a "jelly jar" for a mould dates from the days when recycling was a necessity in working-class families. It is still the best way of retaining the meat juices with the result that, when cold, the loaf is tender and succulent.'

SERVES FOUR

*350g (12oz) steak or mince
  meat*
2 shallots
225g (8oz) smoked ham or
  bacon
50g (2oz) fresh breadcrumbs
¼ teaspoon mace

*¼ teaspoon nutmeg
salt and freshly ground black
  pepper*
1 egg, beaten
*2 tablespoons fried breadcrumbs
  (optional)*

Mince the steak, shallots and ham. Add the fresh breadcrumbs, spices and season with salt and pepper. Stir thoroughly, then mix in the beaten egg. Pack the meat into a 'jelly jar', a cylindrical, pottery jar, such as an old-style marmalade jar (or a pudding basin or loaf tin). Cover first with greaseproof paper, then foil, tie it securely under the rim with string and steam for 2 hours.

Leave to cool, then refrigerate. Run a knife down the inside of the jar and turn the loaf out. Sprinkle the fried breadcrumbs over the loaf to decorate. Slice and serve cold.

AUNT WINNIE'S BEEF ROLL

Mary Pilbery, Potters Bar, Hertfordshire

Aunt Winnie was born at Castle Barnard at the turn of the century, the daughter of the then Station Master of Darlington.

Winnie married Alderman Sanders Hutton and they served as Mayor and Mayoress of Darlington. Her niece, Mary, spent happy summer holidays with her. 'My earliest memories of Aunt Winnie are of a plump, kindly lady welcoming my family to her little stone cottage near Richmond. When we arrived after a long journey in our old and somewhat unreliable BSA car, Aunt Winnie would always make a wonderful, welcoming meal – including her special Beef Roll, which we all loved. Any leftovers would be taken for a picnic up on the Yorkshire moors the next day.'

SERVES FOUR

450g (1lb) minced beef
225g (8oz) minced ham and bacon (mixture of whatever is available)
150g (5oz) breadcrumbs
1 egg
300ml (10fl oz) stock
salt and freshly ground black pepper

Mix all the ingredients together and put them into a heatproof pudding bowl. Cover with foil and steam for 3 hours.

Right: Winnie and Sanders Hutton, 1952.

74

SAUSAGE STOVIES

Marie McLafferty, Glasgow, Scotland

When times were hard in Glasgow's East End, Alice Page found this tasty recipe a great help: it filled bellies without emptying her purse.

Born in Glasgow in 1925, she lost her parents as a teenager and had to raise her three sisters herself. She subsequently married and had four children of her own, and now has nine grandchildren.

She cooked up Sausage Stovies every Friday for years when a family friend came over for supper. The recipe is still a family favourite with her children and grandchildren. Her daughter, Marie, from Glasgow, says: 'When we were small and money was short, mum made this for us. I loved it and still make it today. The kids love it.'

SERVES THREE TO FOUR

850g (2 lb) potatoes
450g (1 lb) onions
6 slices sausage or *sausagemeat*
2 beef stock cubes

Peel and slice the potatoes and then place them in a large saucepan or heatproof pot.

Finely chop the onions and layer over the potatoes. Dice sausage and use this to make a third layer.

Crumble the stock cubes into 600 ml (1 pint) of warm water to make a stock and pour over the ingredients in the pan. Simmer until all the layers blend together in a mash (about 30–40 minutes), stirring it occasionally to stop the mixture sticking.

Alice and Ernest's wedding in 1945.

SCOTCH SCALLOPS

Alison Hulse, Chorley, Lancashire

This recipe is so called because the shape of the potatoes resembles scallops – it is not actually a fish dish!

Alison Hulse from Chorley says that it has been a very popular dish in her family for at least three generations. Her grandmother, Mary, worked in a clothes factory in Wigan and her brother and sisters worked in the cotton mills. She used to cook Scotch Scallops – named, thinks Alison, 'after an old aunt who lived in Scotland and must have first cooked the dish for my grandmother. My grandmother cooked it a lot during the War when it was a staple dish – potatoes were cheap and filling. When rationing ended, she sometimes substituted lamb chops or ham for the bacon, but we prefer bacon.' It is very versatile too – nowadays Alison adds herbs and sometimes sprinkles grated cheese on the top and lets it melt to make a cheesy alternative.

SERVES FOUR

1 tablespoon vegetable oil
8 rashers of bacon
1.5 kg (3½ lb) potatoes
1 large onion
1 teaspoon mixed herbs
salt and freshly ground black
*   pepper*

Heat the oil in a very large frying pan with a lid and fry the bacon, uncovered. Remove the rashers with a slotted spoon to a plate and keep warm.

Peel the potatoes and slice them into thick rounds. Chop the onion and put the pieces into the pan together with the potatoes. Sprinkle with the herbs, salt and pepper to taste and barely cover with water. Cover the pan and simmer for about 20 minutes. Place the bacon on top of the potatoes and onions and cook for 10 more minutes or until the potatoes are cooked through. Serve piping hot.

Alison's mother, aunt and grandparents.

BATE PIE

Thelma Emanuel, North London

Joseph West used to take a Bate Pie down the pit at Waldridge Fell in County Durham around 1900. Bate meant 'meal' and it was an early form of lunch box or take-away – not unlike the Cornish pasty eaten by tin miners in the West Country. The pastry case keeps the contents intact and it is traditionally filled with fresh ingredients and leftovers – nothing went to waste in those days. Joseph's wife, Elizabeth, used to make them for him and one had to keep him going through his long shift.

Sadly, Elizabeth died young. Her granddaughter, Thelma Emanuel, has happy memories of her recipes as her own mother used to bake Bate Pie for special occasions. 'My mother had little money in the twenties and we used to go to the soup kitchens, but my grandmother's recipes were very popular and I particularly remember enjoying this dish when I came home on leave from the WAAF during the War. My mother knew it was a special treat for me. It is always a complete meal and was particularly good in those days when there were odds and ends to finish up that couldn't be wasted. It is very moist and best eaten cold.'

For the shortcrust pastry
75g (3oz) white fat
175g (6oz) flour

For the filling
225g (8oz) potatoes, thickly
   sliced or leftover cooked ones
450g (1lb) leeks, sliced
25g (1oz) butter or margarine
225g (8oz) streaky bacon
2 eggs, hardboiled, thickly sliced
1 egg, beaten
salt and freshly ground black
   pepper

Pre-heat the oven to gas mark 5,
190°C (375°F).

First, make the pastry. Rub the fat
into the flour until the mixture
resembles breadcrumbs. Mix in just
enough cold water (about 1 tablespoon) to form a dough. Turn it out
on to a floured surface and roll out to
a thickness of about 5mm (¼in).

Line a large enamel or ovenproof
china dinner plate with the pastry and
cut out another piece the same size
and shape. This will cover the filling
later.

Next prepare the filling. Parboil the
raw potatoes or slice leftover cooked
ones.

Assemble the prepared filling
ingredients in layers on the pastry-
covered plate. Pour three-quarters of
the beaten egg evenly over the filling.
Cover with the second piece of
pastry, prick here and there and brush
the remaining egg over it. Bake in the
pre-heated oven for about 40 minutes
or until golden brown.

Serve hot or cold – best cold!

Left: Joseph and Elizabeth and their grandchildren.

TATTIE BAKE

Yvonne Hopson, Barnsley, South Yorkshire

This recipe enjoyed a revival in the 1984–5 miner's strike, when it was renamed 'Strike Special'. Yvonne Hopson's husband, Andrew, worked at the North Gawber Colliery, which sadly now no longer exists – it was one of the first pits to close after the strike ended.

Yvonne comes from four generations of mining families: in 1936 her great-uncle, Walter Smith, was killed in the 1936 Wharncliffe Colliery explosion; his brother Tom, Yvonne's grandfather, was also a miner.

The women in these families have always had to provide food for them on a shoestring budget. During the strike she, too, had very little money and she remembered her grandmother Gladys Smith's recipe for Tattie Bake and realized that it was just the thing to feed her family. 'We ate it three or four times a week,' says Yvonne, who was pregnant with her second child at the time. 'My grandmother lived and died in the same street in Barnsley and my mother was one of her 11 children. She was clever at making ends meet and this "throw together" meal was one of the wholesome and filling recipes that kept the family fed. Little did she know how handy her recipe would be 50 years later.'

Yvonne says that the measurements are not exact as it rather depends on what she has to use up, but lots of potatoes are essential!

SERVES FOUR

750g (1½ lb) stewing steak or leftover meat
1 × 500-g (1-lb) packet mixed pulses for soup
300ml (10 fl oz) stock (choose flavour appropriate to meat)
2 large onions, sliced
4 carrots, sliced
1.5 kg (3 lb) potatoes, sliced
100g (4 oz) fresh breadcrumbs
100g (4 oz) cheese, grated
2 tablespoons chopped fresh parsley

Pre-heat the oven to gas mark 4, 180°C (350°F).

If you are using raw meat, seal it by frying it quickly.

Pour the mixed pulses into a large saucepan, add the stock and the meat and simmer gently until the meat is tender (about 1 hour).

Transfer the mixture to a large, ovenproof casserole dish. Add more stock, if necessary, to cover. Mix in the onions and carrots, then cover with the potatoes and top with the breadcrumbs, cheese and, finally, parsley. Cook for about 40 minutes until potatoes are cooked and the top is golden.

Below: Gladys Smith with husband Tom.

MUM'S IMPOSSIBLE PIE

Judith Leacock, South London

This pie was invented by Judith Leacock's mother, Peggy, who was born in Scotland, but emigrated to Australia when she was only three months old. She trained as a nurse in Sydney, married an Australian and had five children.

Peggy was a good cook and expert at just throwing things together when unexpected guests turned up. All her children cook the different versions of this pie and swear it's 100 per cent foolproof! 'The great thing about it is that, as its title suggests, if guests arrive unexpectedly it's impossible not to make a delicious meal from the ingredients in your store cupboard. And it's very adaptable,' says Judith.

SERVES FOUR

Basic mix
4 eggs
475 ml (16 fl oz) milk
75 g (3 oz) plain flour
½ teaspoon baking powder
pinch of salt
100 g (4 oz) margarine, melted

Filling
200 g (7 oz) tinned tuna or *salmon, drained*
1 onion, finely chopped
25 g (1 oz) cheese, grated
freshly ground black pepper

2 tablespoons chopped fresh parsley

Suggestions for other fillings; three savoury and one sweet
200 g (7 oz) cooked or *tinned prawns*
3–4 spring onions or *shallots, sliced*
25 g (1 oz) cheese, shredded

——— • ———

200 g (7 oz) sautéed or *fried and crumbled bacon*
2–3 sliced or *chopped tomatoes*
1 onion, chopped

——— • ———

1 × 425-g (15-oz) tin or *cooked asparagus*
25 g (1 oz) cooked macaroni
25 g (1 oz) cheese, grated

——— • ———

150 g (5 oz) sugar
90 g (3½ oz) desiccated coconut
1–2 teaspoons vanilla essence

Pre-heat the oven to gas mark 5, 190°C (375°F).

Beat the eggs, milk, flour, baking powder, salt and margarine together.

Stir in the chosen filling to make a sweet or savoury pie as desired.

Pour into a lightly greased 25-cm (10-in) pie plate and bake in the pre-heated oven for about 35–40 minutes or until set.

THRIFT PIE

Carole Venner, Bristol, Avon

Kathleen Sims was born in Lancashire in 1923, the fifth child of a cotton mill worker. She married at 18 and quickly found out how to make a penny do the work of a sixpence!

Thursday night was Thrift Pie night, recalls her daughter Carole: 'My mother had always used up her weekly housekeeping money and had to rely on her stores to cook the supper. She liked giving us fresh fruit, salads, stoneground wholemeal bread and pulses – especially butter beans.'

Not only did she work hard to feed her children but she also made their clothes. Carole still remembers going to school in a pinafore dress made from an old coat – the material was so heavy it felt like a strait-jacket!

Kathleen is still making Thrift Pie and, although she invented it over 50 years ago, it is still a convenient and delicious savoury recipe.

SERVES TWO TO THREE

1 onion, finely sliced
1 tablespoon oil
2 slices wholemeal bread
*   crumbled into breadcrumbs*
2 eggs, beaten
300 ml (10 fl oz) milk
50 g (2 oz) Cheddar cheese,
*   grated*
salt and freshly ground black
*   pepper*
2 tomatoes, sliced

Pre-heat the oven to gas mark 4, 180°C (350°F).

Lightly fry the onion in the oil and place in an ovenproof dish.

Cover with the breadcrumbs.

Mix the eggs with the milk and cheese and pour into the dish.

Season to taste with salt and pepper and decorate with the tomato slices.

Bake in the pre-heated oven for 30 minutes.

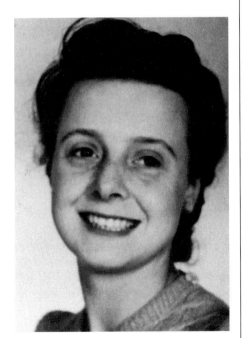

Kathleen Sims.

HERRING AND APPLE PIE

Elizabeth Sinclair, Alloa, Scotland

Grandpa Alex Sinclair was a 'carrier', an early type of haulage contractor long before articulated lorries came into being. The Sinclairs lived in a little cottage overlooking Lybster Harbour in Caithness around 1850. There, he used to carry goods between Wick and Thurso on his horse and cart.

'He used to own a whisky still and was often paid unwelcome visits from the Customs and Excise men,' says Elizabeth Sinclair, who is married to Grandpa Alex's great-grandson. 'Fortunately, Grannie Sinclair was a very hospitable woman and somehow the Customs men always tended to "forget" about the whisky – thanks to her home cooking and baking!'

Herring and Apple Pie always had pride of place on the table at family parties, surrounded by the dropped scones, treacle scones, oat cakes and cheese. The clootie dumpling followed, with a piece of shortbread and a cup of tea!

The pie is still enjoyed by the Sinclairs: 'It's one of those hand-me-down recipes that calls for "a hanfu' o' this and a hanfu' o' that",' says Elizabeth. In those days, herrings were plentiful and cheap and were usually cooked with oatmeal and tatties (potatoes!). The pie is now enjoyed by Alex's great-great-granddaughters who live in London and who have mastered the art of baking the pie for parties – especially for Hogmanay – so the recipe is assured a long life.

SERVES SIX

For the shortcrust pastry
175g (6oz) flour
pinch of salt
50g (2oz) margarine

For the filling
6 herrings, filleted,
1 onion, sliced
2 cooking apples, sliced
300ml (10fl oz) cider
large pinch of mixed herbs
salt and freshly ground black
  pepper
1 egg, beaten

Pre-heat the oven to gas mark 7, 220°C (425°F).

First, make the pastry. Mix the flour and salt together in a mixing bowl. Rub the margarine into the flour until the mixture resembles breadcrumbs, then mix in just enough

Below: The Sinclair Family (Alex is on the right).

cold water to make a dough (about 1 tablespoon). Roll out the pastry on a lightly floured surface until it is large enough to cover a 20-cm (8-in) diameter pie dish and there is quite a large margin. Grease the dish and press it on to the pastry so you know how much you need to top the pie, then cut out fish shapes from the rest to decorate the pie later.

Now make the filling. Place the herrings and other ingredients in the prepared pie dish, distributing them evenly, then cover with the pastry, trim and decorate with the pastry fishes. Make a hole in the centre of the pastry lid. Brush with the beaten egg. Bake in the pre-heated oven until the pastry is golden brown (about 20–25 minutes).

AUNTIE'S STEAMED SALMON SOUFFLÉ

Louise Boreham, Burntisland, Fife, Scotland

This is another recipe from Margaret Wilson's collection (see page 43 for her Chocolate Biscuit Cake), sent by her stepdaughter Louise Boreham. During the Second World War Margaret worked wonders with the scant wartime rations. Precious brown packets of sugar were carefully hoarded to make jams and jellies with whatever fruits they could find in the countryside. 'Occasionally, as a special treat, she got a scraggy shank of mutton, used it to flavour soup and then scraped off the meat and added mashed potato and carrot to make rissoles. Vegetables were always available from my father's allotment, which involved a minor excursion a mile away along the tow-path of the Union Canal,' remembers Louise.

Rationing continued long after the War, but Margaret's other sister had married a Canadian seaman and so the family received regular food parcels from Canada. 'How we used to long for those parcels as they usually contained packets of Jello, Chiclets and Lifebuoys [sweets] and – the best treat of all – a tin of salmon, which Margaret would turn into the most wonderful soufflé, using our precious rationed eggs. The soufflé was such a delicacy that we ate it in tiny slivers to prolong the ecstasy!'

SERVES FOUR

1 × 213-g (7-oz) tin red salmon
50g (2oz) brown breadcrumbs
salt and freshly ground black
  pepper
2 eggs

Tip the tinned salmon into a bowl, remove any skin and bones and break the fish up into chunks. Mix in the breadcrumbs and season to taste.

Separate the egg yolks from the whites and mix the yolks well into the salmon and breadcrumb mixture.

Whip the whites until they are stiff and fold carefully into the salmon mixture. Grease a heatproof pudding bowl, tip the mixture in, and smooth the surface. Cover the top with greaseproof paper and a cloth and tie securely under the rim with string.

Steam for 1 hour, ensuring that the water level neither comes over the top of the bowl nor falls too low.

Serve in wedges with parsley sauce, new potatoes and garden peas or, for real luxury, asparagus.

Below: Louise with Aunt Margaret (right) and a friend in 1944.

FALSE FISH

Madalaine Brady, Bangor, Gwynedd, Wales

False Fish was invented by Beatrice Lord just after the First World War. Her husband, Jack, worked in a Lancashire cotton mill before the War, but returned from the Front to find that there was no longer a job for him there. As there were seven hungry children to feed and very little money, Beatrice had to be very resourceful. At one time, she didn't even have a proper oven, but still managed to bake wonderful things in an old biscuit tin over a gas ring!

Beatrice's granddaughter, Madalaine Brady, remembers her as 'always looking very elegant, even though she hardly had two pennies to rub together'.

Beatrice named this dish 'False Fish' because when cooked and sliced, it resembles fish steaks. She entered it for a competition held at the local clinic to find 'a nourishing family meal for less than a shilling', and won. The prize? A shilling!

Adding an onion to a recipe was a treat in those days as, apparently, they were scarce in the First World War. So much so that in another raffle at the local Conservative Club, the first prize was an onion!

Madalaine Brady still makes false fish today because 'It's so simple, looks wonderful and is adaptable to individual tastes. It also keeps people guessing as to the ingredients.'

SERVES FOUR

200g (7oz) long- or short-grain rice
200g (7oz) red lentils
1 clove garlic, chopped
1 onion, chopped (optional)
3 tablespoons herbs of your choice
pinch of salt
1 egg, beaten
100g (4oz) fresh breadcrumbs
oil for frying

Boil the rice in plenty of water until cooked (about 20 minutes).

Meanwhile, cook the lentils, garlic and onion, if using, together in as little water as possible.

As soon as the rice and lentils are just cooked, drain them and stir them together, adding the herbs and salt, and press into a 1.2-litre (2-pint) pudding basin. Fit a saucer into the basin, on top of the mixture, weight it down and leave overnight (Beatrice used a flat iron but a couple of tins work well, too).

The following day, remove the weight(s) and saucer, unmould the mixture and cut into slices. Coat the slices with egg, then breadcrumbs and fry until golden brown.

Serve with fresh vegetables and parsley sauce.

Right: Beatrice Lord.

MOCK GOOSE

Cynthia Smith, Coventry, Warwickshire

Cynthia Smith's mother was one of many British housewives who, during the Second World War, were brilliantly inventive and adaptive. They kept their families happy and in good health despite the deprivations of the time *and* they produced recipes that have remained firm favourites ever since.

'As children growing up in Yorkshire, Mock Goose was my mother's speciality, which, though born of war-time necessity, was one of those ideas that are simply brilliant because they are so wonderfully simple. As long as my father, an enthusiastic gardener, produced the apples and potatoes on his war-time plot and dried the herbs, this recipe used only *one* rationed ingredient – cheese (usually imported – a real treat!).'

These days Cynthia uses the best possible ingredients and this war-time recipe has become a family favourite. It is perfect for vegetarians for despite the name, the dish is meatless.

SERVES THREE TO FOUR

450g (1 lb) potatoes, diced
450g (1 lb) cooking apples
(preferably Bramleys), diced
450g (1 lb) onions, diced
250g (9 oz) cheese (preferably
extra mature Cheddar), diced

5 tablespoons chopped fresh or
2½ tablespoons dried sage
salt and freshly ground black
pepper

For the topping
50–100g (2–4 oz) dried
breadcrumbs or sage and onion
stuffing mix
50g (2 oz) cheese, grated

Pre-heat the oven to gas mark 5, 190°C (375°F).

Toss the potatoes, apples, onion, cheese and sage together, seasoning with salt and pepper, until they are well mixed. Turn the mixture into a large, buttered ovenproof dish, cover (with a lid, foil or buttered grease-proof paper) and bake for about 30 minutes or until the vegetables and fruit are really tender.

Meanwhile, mix together the topping ingredients (Cynthia says she usually cheats and uses a good proprietary brand of sage and onion stuffing).

When the 30 minutes have elapsed, uncover the dish, sprinkle the topping liberally over the dish and return to the oven, raising the temperature to gas mark 9, 240°C (475°F), for 10 more minutes or until just nicely browned.

Serve with a mixed green salad and crusty, wholemeal bread.

RECIPES FROM ABROAD

ESTONIAN SPRING MILK SOUP 92
CATHRINE'S PARTY SOLE 93
SALT COD WITH VEGETABLES 94
BARBECUED BAKED BEANS 96
BEEF OLIVES 97
SPECIAL PERSIAN MIXED RICE 98
PUMPKIN AU FOUR 100
CHICOREE D'ENFANCE AU GRATIN 101
BABA'S POLENTA 102
AUBERGINE AFGHANI 104
MESSODA'S CAULIFLOWER 105

•

GERMAN APPLE TORTE 106
APPLE CAKE ERNST 108
GRANDMA DELLA'S APPLE COCOA CAKE 110
GRANDMA SUMMERS'
RHUBARB CUSTARD PIE 111
MRS CARLTON'S FAVOURITE PECAN PIE 112
GATEAU AU CHOCOLAT MAMAN 113
BAKED FUDGE PUDDING 114
WACKY CHOCOLATE CAKE 116
NUT AND CHOCOLATE CREAM GATEAU 118
FRUIT LOAF 120
EMPEROR'S SOUFFLE 121
STUFFED MONKEY 122
FRUIT SALAD MOULD 123
CINNAMON BALLS 124
PLONS FREDDO 126

ESTONIAN SPRING MILK SOUP

Helve Bateman, Uttoxeter, Staffordshire

Marina and Evald Sidron met in a Displaced Persons Camp in Germany during the Second World War. When the War ended, they came to England and another camp, near Uttoxeter in Staffordshire.

They married shortly afterwards and Evald found work on local farms. He had been brought up on a farm in Estonia where life was very simple. There may have been very little money, but there was no lack of fresh vegetables.

'My parents were always busy when I was growing up and when I was about eleven it often fell to me to cook the main meal. My father taught me to make this simple, but delicious soup. It didn't take me that long to make,' writes their daughter, Helve. 'It tastes best with fresh spring vegetables, but can be made all the year round.'

SERVES THREE TO FOUR

*450 ml (15 fl oz) fresh vegetable
   stock (or use a vegetable stock
   cube)*
2–3 medium carrots
2–4 new potatoes
*100 g (4 oz) shelled young peas
   or frozen peas*
600 ml (1 pint) milk

*salt and freshly ground black
   pepper*
knob of butter
few chives, chopped, to garnish

Bring the stock to the boil in a large saucepan. Cut the carrots into 4 pieces lengthways, then finely slice across and add to the boiling stock. Simmer for about 5 minutes until the carrots are just beginning to cook.

Meanwhile, scrape the new potatoes, cut into small dice and add to the stock. Simmer gently for 4 more minutes until they are just beginning to cook. Skim the froth off the surface of the stock.

Add the peas to the pan and simmer everything very gently – the potatoes must not overcook and begin to break up, nor must the soup burn (there will not be much spare stock with all the vegetables in the pan).

Add the milk, bring slowly back to the boil, seasoning to taste with salt and pepper. Just before it is about to boil over, take the pan off the heat and stir in the butter. Cover with the lid and leave for 5 minutes in a warm place for the flavours to mingle. Serve garnished with the chives and fresh, crusty buttered bread.

Note You can add other vegetables such as leeks to the soup for variety.

CATHRINE'S PARTY SOLE

Evelyn Grant, Old Portsmouth, Hampshire

Cathrine Cadoret was born in Paris in 1881, the daughter of an English mother and a French father. 'She was tall, blue-eyed with a mass of lovely, long, dark hair,' says Evelyn Grant, the cousin she met in 1926 when Cathrine visited her English relations in London. Cathrine stayed for several years and cooked marvellous meals for them. 'When my mother gave dinner parties, Cathrine would be prevailed upon to make something special and this recipe was always a great success,' recalls Evelyn.

Cathrine returned to Paris and, during the Second World War, was a member of the Resistance Movement under the German Occupation.

She never married, but Evelyn often took her sons to stay at her flat near the Eiffel Tower and they all have very happy memories of those times.

SERVES FOUR

225 g (8 oz) frozen puff pastry, defrosted
4 fillets Dover sole, skinned
salt and freshly ground black pepper

25 g (1 oz) butter
few sprigs of fresh dill, chopped, a few fronds reserved to garnish
150 ml (5 fl oz) thick double cream
crab apple jelly to taste

Pre-heat the oven to gas mark 7, 220°C (425°F).

Roll out the pastry to a 5-mm (¼-in) thickness and cut into 4 rounds, each 10 cm (4 in) in diameter. Bake in the pre-heated oven until brown and crisp.

Season each fillet of sole, place a small knob of butter in the middle of each piece and roll up. Place the fillets on a buttered, heatproof plate, cover with a domed lid and steam over gently simmering water for about 15 minutes.

Lift the fish off the plate with a slotted spoon so that it drains well and place each one on a piece of pastry. Strain the liquid left on the plate into a small saucepan, add the dill and cream to it and boil until thick. Pour the sauce over the fish and pastry. Put a small blob of crab apple jelly on each and decorate with the reserved dill fronds. Serve at once.

SALT COD WITH VEGETABLES

Stuart Martinson, Swansea, West Glamorgan, Wales

Martin Martinson was born in 1877 and lived in Estonia, but was of Danish origin – his father was the Consul to Estonia at the time. He ran away to sea at the age of 14, eventually came ashore in Cardiff around 1900 and decided to stay. He was appointed chef at the Park Hotel in Cardiff where he fell in love with the assistant chef, who was a Welsh

Below left: Martin Martinson.

girl from Rhayader called Catherine Davis. They married in 1900.

According to their grandson, Stuart Martinson, there were attempts by Martin's family to get him to go back to his family: 'A couple of years after their marriage a member of Martin's family was sent to Wales to take the young couple back, but my great-grandmother refused to let her daughter go!'

Martin always referred to this fish recipe as 'toe-rag', which is not, perhaps, the most complimentary name for such an appetizing dish. It is a cheap, nutritious dish that is very easy to make and it has survived both the test of time and a trip from the Baltic.

SERVES FOUR

375 g (13 oz) salt cod (available from Spanish, Portuguese and West Indian shops)
450 ml (15 fl oz) milk
15 g (½ oz) butter
3 tablespoons chopped fresh parsley
freshly ground black pepper
150 ml (5 fl oz) single cream
salt, if necessary

Soak the cod overnight in about 300 ml (10 fl oz) of the milk.

Drain the milk from the cod and discard it. Rinse the fish under cold running water (how long you rinse will depend on the fish − rinse for longer if the fish is very salty). Pat the cod dry and place on a large, round heatproof plate. Pour 1 tablespoon of milk over each cutlet, then place a small knob of butter on each piece of fish. Sprinkle each with about 1 tablespoon of the parsley and pepper to taste.

Half fill a large saucepan − big enough to rest the rim of the plate on − with water and bring it to the boil. Place the plate over the top of the saucepan and then put the saucepan lid over the plate, covering the fish completely. Reduce the heat to a fast simmer and leave *without raising the lid* for about 30–40 minutes or until cooked.

Remove the fish from the plate and keep it warm. Strain the plate juices into a saucepan and, over a medium heat, add the remaining tablespoon of parsley and some or all of the cream and stir to thicken. Season with black pepper (salt may be added at this point if you wish, but is usually not necessary).

Spoon the sauce over the fish and serve with mashed potatoes and fresh green vegetables (although originally this dish would have been served with pickled vegetables).

BARBECUED BAKED BEANS

Joan Hunt, York, Yorkshire

Lilian Valentine was born in Baltimore, USA in 1897. She was still in her teens when she met Edward Valentine, who, at 17, was lying about his age and attempting to enlist in the First World War. They married and, in 1920, left the East Coast to go West, to Tacoma in Washington State.

Lilian in 1922.

She had six children and became a keen cook and, for those days, a very unusual one. She learned Italian recipes and then switched to Chinese ones. Lilian's knowledge of these cuisines led her to experiment with spices and sauces not readily available in American stores in the 1930s and 1940s. Thus, her recipe for Barbecued Baked Beans contains soy sauce and chilli powder, which give it a good kick, according to her granddaughter Joan Hunt.

SERVES SIX

450g (1 lb) dried haricot beans
225g (½ lb) salt pork or bacon ends, cut into small pieces
1 large onion, sliced
100–120g (4–4½ oz) brown sugar
1 × 142g (5 oz) tin tomato purée
1 × 793g (1 lb 12 oz) tin chopped tomatoes
2 cloves garlic, chopped
2 tablespoons soy sauce
1 teaspoon chilli powder
1 teaspoon allspice
1 teaspoon mustard powder
salt, to taste

Soak the beans overnight in cold water.

Next morning, drain and rinse them. Place the beans in a large saucepan and add all the other ingredients, plus just enough water to cover them. Cook on the hob over the lowest heat or bake in the oven at gas mark 2, 150°C (300°F) for 3½–4 hours or until the beans are tender. Add salt to taste after 1–2 hours and add more water then if it is necessary. Also, be sure to stir often towards the end of the cooking time to prevent the beans sticking.

BEEF OLIVES

Charlene Ives, Letchworth, Hertfordshire

Michalena Urbanaski was born in Poland in 1888 and lived outside Warsaw until she emigrated to America with her sister in 1910. She settled in Chicago, married and had six children.

'Grandmother was an excellent cook and did it all without a cookbook,' says Charlene Ives, one of Michalena's granddaughters, who knew her methods well as she lived with her until she was 14. 'She used to make whisky for her husband Frank during the days of Prohibition. She would seal up the windows and doors, erect a still and proceed to make the liquor. One day it blew up and she was almost caught.'

Once, when Michalena was staying with Charlene's other grandmother, she offered to cook a meal. 'On the mantelpiece was a jar, which she thought was pepper, so she put plenty in the stew. When my other grandmother returned home, she informed her that the pepper was, in fact, the ashes of my paternal grandfather! I believe the stew had been eaten by this time.'

'This recipe is special because it is tender, tasty and can be made in advance. It is especially nice if you serve it with mashed potatoes and fresh vegetables.'

SERVES FOUR

1.5 kg (3 lb) steak, sliced
450 g (1 lb) lean smoked bacon
flour, for dusting and thickening
olive oil, for frying
2 medium onions, chopped
½ green pepper, deseeded
2 cloves garlic, crushed
2 sticks celery
8 small mushrooms
300 ml (10 fl oz) water
salt and freshly ground black
pepper

Pre-heat the oven to gas mark 4, 180°C (350°F).

Lay a piece of bacon on a steak, roll it up and tie with string. Roll in flour. Brown each parcel in olive oil heated in a flameproof casserole, then put aside. Brown the onion in the same pot, then put aside. Cut the green pepper into thin strips and lightly fry with the garlic in the same pot. Slice the celery and mushrooms and add to the pot. Return everything to the pot. Add the water and season to taste with salt and pepper. Cover and bake for 2½ hours or until tender.

Strain off the gravy and thicken with a little flour.

Serve with mashed potatoes and fresh vegetables.

SPECIAL PERSIAN MIXED RICE

Debbie Hughson, Edinburgh, Scotland

Abdul Rasool Zareian originally came from the small village of Jahrom in South West Iran. He went to catering college and had to do a lot of cooking during his two years' National Service.

In the late 1940s, Abdul went to live in the Gulf States and opened several small stores. He turned down the opportunity to own a large piece of land in the Gulf for a small outlay: 'Had he bought the land, he would now be very rich as oil was discovered there some years later!', laments his daughter, Debbie.

Abdul – known as Ali – came to Birmingham about 30 years ago. For the first two years, he had little money and virtually lived on his Special Persian Mixed Rice as it was cheap and tasty. 'I love cooking this dish and I hope to master many more delicious Persian dishes to pass on to my own children,' says Debbie.

Abdul Zareian in 1971.

100g (4oz) butter
750g (1½lb) stewing lamb, cut
  into bite-sized chunks
1 large onion, chopped
2 teaspoons turmeric
1 teaspoon cumin seeds
3-cm (1-in) piece cinnamon stick
1 black or 5 green cardamom
  pods
5 whole cloves
3 garlic cloves, chopped
3-cm (1-in) piece root ginger,
  peeled and finely chopped or
  grated
2 small fresh chillies, finely
  chopped
2 teaspoons black pepper
1 × 397-g (14-oz) tin chopped
  tomatoes
300ml (10fl oz) stock
225g (8oz) basmati rice
salt to taste

Melt the butter in a large pan that has
a very close-fitting lid (if you cannot
get a perfect seal, wrap a cloth or tea
towel around the lid but keep well
clear of the cooker top) and brown
the meat and onions. Add all the
other ingredients except for the
tomatoes, stock, rice and salt. Stir
them in gently and cook over a low
heat for 2–3 minutes.

Gradually add the chopped
tomatoes, stirring all the time. Add
half of the stock and simmer for 30–
45 minutes until the meat has cooked.

Rinse the rice until the water runs
clear, then drain. Add it to the pan
with the remaining stock, plus salt to
taste, and stir. You should have a
sloppy mixture, but if it is too stiff,
add a little more water. Cover (using
your tea towel if necessary) and cook
gently for 20 minutes. At this point,
check to see that all the liquid has
been absorbed. If it is still wet, cook
for a little longer, uncovered.
However, if the rice is still not quite
cooked, add some more water and
cook for a little longer, covered.

Serve with a mixed green salad,
without a dressing, and a side dish of
cucumber, mint and yoghurt.

PUMPKIN AU FOUR

Mireille Ellington, South East London

Jean Baptiste Mathieu was born around 1840 and was a shepherd in the region of Sisteron in the French Alps. Every year he would go down the mountains to Provence in the South of France to seek seasonal work. One year he met a girl called Fortunée Bellon, the daughter of a local farmer, fell in love and married her. They had seven children.

Jean Baptiste enjoyed cooking in their shepherd's cottage and for this recipe, one of his favourite dishes, used pumpkin, eggs and cheese. His great-great-granddaughter, Mireille Ellington (who married an English-man and now lives in London), says it is an old family joke that Jean Baptiste's courtship of Mademoiselle Bellon must have been helped by his delicious recipe for pumpkin. 'It looks and smells marvellous, and tastes wonderful on a chilly autumn evening,' says Mireille.

SERVES SIX

1 pumpkin (at least 30 cm/12 in
    in diameter)
4 hardboiled eggs, shelled and
    finely chopped
1 bunch of fresh parsley, chopped
4 cloves garlic crushed
salt and freshly ground black
    pepper
150g (5 oz) fresh breadcrumbs

450g (1 lb) cheese (Cheddar,
    Emmental or Jarlsberg), grated
150 ml (5 fl oz) double cream

Pre-heat the oven to gas mark 6, 200°C (400°F).

Take the pumpkin and cut out a large circle around the stalk (about 15 cm/6 in in diameter). Pull out the circle and keep to use as a lid later. Remove the seeds and the stringy mesh from inside the pumpkin until the pumpkin is empty, leaving, approximately, a 1-cm (½-in) thick wall all around.

Chop the scrapings coarsely and add to them the egg, parsley and garlic. Add salt and plenty of pepper.

Using the pumpkin shell as a dish, spread a layer of the pumpkin mixture over the bottom and press down well, then a layer of breadcrumbs, then a layer of grated cheese. Repeat until you are about 1 cm (½ in) from the top. Now pour the double cream into the hole and close the opening with the reserved pumpkin lid.

Place the filled pumpkin in a baking dish and bake for 2 hours (allow more time depending on the size of your pumpkin).

Remove from the oven and place on an earthenware dish in the centre of the table. Only fresh brown bread and white wine should accompany this dish.

CHICOREE D'ENFANCE AU GRATIN

Alexander Janssen, South East London

Madeleine Jeanne de Moulin was born in 1919 in the Loire Valley. Her son Alexander often cooks this rich chicory dish of hers: 'It is very special to me – it is economic, easy to make and delicious. Above all it reminds me of my childhood and of my mother.'

SERVES FOUR

8 heads (about 850g/2lb)
   chicory
olive oil, for frying
freshly ground black pepper
pinch of freshly ground nutmeg
8 slices honey roast ham
350g (12oz) Gruyère or
   Emmental cheese, grated

'Robert' Sauce
50g (2oz) butter
2 onions, sliced
1 clove garlic, chopped
1 tablespoon flour
300ml (10fl oz) stock
150ml (5fl oz) milk
bouquet garni (tie sprig of thyme,
   1 bay leaf and a few
   peppercorns in a square of
   muslin)
salt and freshly ground black
   pepper
1 teaspoon Dijon mustard
1 teaspoon vinegar
1 teaspoon lemon juice

Prepare the chicory for cooking: cut off the hard ends, strip off any damaged leaves and scoop out the core. Boil in slightly salted water until tender (about 5–10 minutes) then drain very thoroughly, letting any water evaporate.

Stir-fry the chicory in some olive oil – adding pepper and the nutmeg – until golden brown and thoroughly cooked. Then, roll each head of chicory up in a slice of ham. Lay the rolls next to each other in an oven-proof dish. Set aside in a warm place.

Next, make the sauce. Melt the butter and fry the onion and garlic in it over a gentle heat until they are golden brown (about 10 minutes). Stir in the flour to form a roux, then very gradually stir in the stock and the milk and bring to the boil, stirring all the time. Add the bouquet garni and a pinch of salt. Cover and simmer for about 30 minutes. Also, set the oven to gas mark 7, 220°C (425°F).

Remove the bouquet garni, stir in the mustard, vinegar and lemon juice and a little salt and pepper to taste, then pour the sauce over the rolls. Sprinkle the grated cheese over the dish, covering it thickly. Bake in the pre-heated oven for about 45 minutes, when the cheese has browned and is bubbling. Top it off with some fresh parsley and serve with potato croquettes and a 1947 claret!

BABA'S POLENTA

Linda Khatir, Dartmouth, Devon

Malek Khatir was born in Tehran in the 1920s. He was educated in Paris, Belgium and Switzerland and he became a Doctor of Law. Malek was a politician in Iran before the Revolution, so, when the Shah was overthrown, Malek fled to Paris.

His daughter-in-law, Linda Khatir, says that Malek is a cosmopolitan gourmet who loves cooking and his basic Middle-Eastern dishes have been influenced by both Italian and French cooking. 'When we were newly-weds living in Paris, we were very poor, living in a tiny studio. My husband was a student, I was an *au pair*

Below left: Baba Khatir.

and we had no money to spare on anything but the basic necessities. Malek would arrive at midday with a steaming parcel containing a delicious lunch for us. Each day it was something different! My favourite dish of all was "Baba's Polenta" – it's simple and filling and always conjures up those romantic memories each time I prepare it.' The recipe that follows is a simplified version of Malek's own. Incidentally, for the curious, 'Baba' means 'Daddy' in Persian.

SERVES SIX TO EIGHT

1 tablespooon oil
1 × 70-g (3-oz) tin double concentrate tomato purée
1 tablespoon chopped fresh parsley
1 tablespoon chopped baby gherkins
salt and freshly ground black pepper
1 × 397-g (14-oz) tin chopped tomatoes (optional)
2 large onions, finely chopped
50g (2oz) butter
450g (1lb) thick-cut smoked bacon, diced
1 × 450-g (1-lb) packet quick-cook polenta
finely grated Gruyère cheese, to garnish

First make the sauce. Heat the oil, add the tomato purée and mix in the parsley, gherkins and season with salt and pepper. Stir over a gentle heat for 1 minute.

Add 600 ml (1 pint) of boiling water, bring the sauce back to the boil, then simmer and stir until the sauce reduces enough to thicken a little. (If you want to make the sauce go further, add the tinned tomatoes at the same time as the water.) Keep warm.

Now, make the polenta. Gently fry the onions in the butter until they have turned golden brown and caramelized. Remove them from the pan and dry-fry the bacon until crisp. Remove from the pan and keep to one side with the onions.

Bring about 2.25 litres (4 pints) lightly salted water to the boil in a large, non-stick saucepan. Pour the contents of the packet of polenta into the boiling water in a steady stream and stir in well. Simmer and stir constantly for 15 minutes. Then, the polenta should have a thick, dough-like consistency.

Remove the pan from the heat and stir in the bacon and onions. Spoon the mixture on to a warmed platter to form a domed shape. Sprinkle the cheese over the top.

Serve with the tomato sauce and a crisp, green salad.

AUBERGINE AFGHANI

Polly Laidler, Wickham Bishops, Essex

Polly Laidler made friends with a diplomatic Afghani family, the Neckos, while she was living in Kuwait. When Anoir Necko was recalled to Afghanistan, his wife Nooria followed, but they asked the Laidlers if they would 'adopt' two of their children, Moulo and Omar, having made the agonizing decision to leave them behind in Kuwait, away from the Communist revolution in Afghanistan.

For two years, Polly Laidler heard nothing from Afghanistan: 'None of us knew if the parents and the other two children were alive, although we had heard various reports. We learnt at first-hand the heartaches and courage of people dispossessed of their country, culture and family members. I learned many of their national dishes, which are now in our family repertoire. Moulo loved cooking her national dishes for us. This dish is one of our favourites – it looks gorgeous and tastes fantastic.'

Eventually, the family escaped to England where they all got back together again and stayed with the Laidlers in Essex.

A few years ago, the Neckos went to live in the USA to try to make a new life. Unfortunately the two families have now lost touch. 'I'd be overjoyed to see them again,' says Polly.

SERVES FOUR

2 slim aubergines
1 tablespoon fresh or *dried mint*
2 large cloves garlic, crushed
1 × 150-g (5-oz) carton natural
 set yoghurt
olive oil, for frying
1 tablespoon thick tomato juice
 or thinned tomato purée

Peel and cut the aubergines into 5-mm (¼-in) thick slices, placing them immediately in salted water (it extracts any bitterness and prevents discolouration). Leave them to soak while you beat the mint and garlic into the yoghurt, then set this mixture aside so the flavours develop.

Heat some oil in a frying pan while you pat the aubergine slices dry between tea towels. Fry the slices in small batches, turning until they brown on both sides. Drain each batch on kitchen paper and arrange on a large serving dish in concentric, overlapping circles. Keep warm. After the last slice is out, pour out some of the oil so you have about 120 ml (4 fl oz) left, then stir in the tomato juice or purée. Do not worry that they will not blend together.

To serve, swirl the yoghurt mixture over the aubergine slices and drizzle the oil and tomato mix over the top in strands or blobs. Serve hot or cold.

MESSODA'S CAULIFLOWER

Adele Geras, Manchester

'I have never tasted anything like this anywhere else but in my family, and I think it's a delicious way to cook cauliflower. It tastes even better the next day – if you can be patient enough!'

Messoda Weston was born in Rabat, Morocco, and married an English trader, Saul Weston. They lived for many years in Egypt and Palestine, until Saul's death. In the late 1940s Messoda went to live in Cardiff with her daughter, Vivienne.

Adele Geras used to stay with her aunt and grandmother in Cardiff in the holidays and has fond memories of those visits: 'Messoda hardly ever went out, but told me the most marvellous stories as she cooked exotic dishes in the tiny little kitchen. She never looked at a recipe book, her frying pan had lost its handle and she preferred to eat alone.' Her cauliflower dish has, however, become a family classic. 'Quantities are approximate . . . if the egg was used up before the cauliflower was all fried, she would crack another; if the frying pan looked dryish, she would add some more oil without drawing breath; if the flour ran out, she would tip some more out over the table. The green stalks lining the bottom of the pan were what she usually ate . . . and they, too, are quite delicious.'

SERVES EIGHT

2 large cauliflowers, divided into florets (retain the green stalks – wash and chop them)
2 large eggs, beaten
120g (4½oz) plain flour, plus extra if necessary
salt and freshly ground black pepper
6 tablespoons sunflower oil (sometimes a little more!)
juice of 3 lemons
50ml (2fl oz) water

Prepare the cauliflower florets by, first, dipping them in the beaten egg, then in the flour, seasoned with salt and pepper.

Heat the oil in a frying pan until it is sizzling, then add the florets. Fry a few at a time until they are a lovely golden brown.

Line the bottom of a heatproof casserole dish with the reserved cauliflower greens, then remove the cooked florets, with a slotted spoon, to the dish, arranging them on top of the chopped stalks. Pour the lemon juice and water over the top, cover and gently simmer for about 20 minutes. Season to taste.

This is wonderful served with a roast and potatoes of any kind or, as Adele recommends, serve it cold the next day.

GERMAN APPLE TORTE

Catherine Scovell, Farnham, Surrey

Freda Behlmer was born around 1860 in Bremen, Germany. After her marriage to Henry, the young couple emigrated to San Francisco as friends had spoken of the marvellous opportunities there and the wonderful location. The journey must have been an extremely long and arduous undertaking as, of course, there was no Panama Canal in those days.

Henry went into the brewing business soon after arriving, but the brewery was damaged in the great earthquake and fire of 1906. 'I remember my grandmother, who was a teenager at the time of the earthquake, telling me stories of those traumatic days . . . She used to say how they had to camp out as their home had been destroyed. She was one of 13 children born to Henry and Freda so it must have been quite a struggle,' writes Freda's great-granddaughter, Catherine.

However, the catastrophe spurred Henry to open his own brewery, which flourished . . . until the years of Prohibition put an end to such enterprises and forced him into retirement.

Freda was, by all accounts, an excellent cook and ran a warm and loving home for her large family. Catherine never knew her great-grandmother, but her father remembers their large family gatherings. There was always plenty of delicious food on the table – including the famous German Apple Torte. This tradition lives on in Catherine's own home (she married an Englishman and has lived in Surrey for 20 years): 'Freda's dessert is perfect for a party or large gathering as it is quite large and rich, but everyone enjoys it and it reminds me of my grandmother.'

SERVES EIGHT

7 large green apples, peeled and
   sliced, but not too thinly
25g (1oz) butter, plus extra for
   greasing
65g (2½oz) brown sugar, plus
   1 tablespoon
7 eggs
500ml (17fl oz) sour cream
2 teaspoons vanilla essence
pinch of salt
1 × 200-g (7-oz) packet French
   toasts

1 tablespoon ground cinnamon
50g (2oz) nuts (walnuts,
   almonds), chopped

Place the apples, butter and brown sugar (reserving 1 tablespoon of it) in a saucepan and gently simmer them together, covered, for 15 minutes

Beat the eggs, sour cream, vanilla essence and salt together in a bowl, then add to the apples, after the 15 minutes have elapsed, and simmer slowly until the mixture thickens, stirring constantly.

Pre-heat the oven to gas mark 2, 150°C (300°F).

Crumble the French toasts to make reasonably uniform, fine crumbs, but take care not to turn them into powder. Sweeten with the remaining brown sugar and the cinnamon.

Thoroughly grease a 25-cm (10-in) loose-bottomed cake tin and line it evenly with the toast crumbs. Pour in the apple mixture and cover evenly with the remaining crumbs. Dot the top with small pieces of butter and then sprinkle the chopped nuts over. Bake in the pre-heated oven for about 45 minutes. Let the Torte cool before serving.

Left: Freda Behlmer with two of her daughters Alma and Anne.
Anne (right) is Catherine's grandmother.

107

APPLE CAKE ERNST

Marianne Walter, Macclesfield, Cheshire

Ernst Jordan was born in Hamm, West Germany in 1903. His cousin, Marianne, came from the same town and is now in her eighties, living in Cheshire.

Marianne studied to become an architect and was one of the last two Jewish students allowed to graduate from the Technical University of Berlin in 1935. Most of her immediate family fled Germany and Nazi persecution in the mid 1930s. Marianne herself escaped to England in 1938. Ernst, meanwhile, trained and began working as a chef for the Hamburg–American shipping line, until Hitler put an end to his career at sea. Both his parents died at the Teresienstadt and Auschwitz concentration camps, but Ernst managed to escape to Palestine.

Ernst became very successful and ran his own hotel and he became a Government adviser on tourism. He left Israel in 1967 to open his own restaurant in Hilversum, Holland, where his apple cake became famous.

Fifty years after they had lost touch with each other, Ernst tracked Marianne down in England and they met again in 1982: 'We met in the airport lounge at Eindhoven – I recognized him immediately, he looked just like my uncle,' recalls Marianne. 'He was very ugly but also very charming!'

Below left: Ernst Jordan.

They rekindled their friendship – so special because no one else in their family who had remained in Germany had survived. Ernst cooked apple cake for Marianne and it is named in his honour.

For the filling
*1 kg (2¼ lb) fine dessert apples
(Cox's, say), cored, peeled
and very finely sliced
50g (2oz) currants
50g (2oz) sultanas
75g (3oz) almonds (preferably
new season's steeped in near
boiling water, peeled and
finely chopped)
juice and finely grated peel of
1 large lemon
2 tablespoons cane or demerara
sugar
1 tablespoon ground cinnamon*

For the pastry
*275g (10oz) self-raising flour
175g (6oz) butter, softened
75g (3oz) sugar
1 large or 2 small eggs
small handful of breadcrumbs or
medium matzo meal*

For the glaze
*2 tablespoons milk
2 tablespoons apricot jam, melted*

Mix all the filling ingredients well and leave to stand overnight.

The next day, make the pastry. Mix all the ingredients, except the breadcrumbs or matzo meal, together to form a firm dough. Rest the dough for 2 hours, wrapped in cling film and put in the refrigerator. Just before this time has elapsed, pre-heat the oven to gas mark 6, 200°C (400°F).

Roll the pastry out to a thickness of about 5mm (¼in).

Grease and flour a 23-cm (9-in) loose bottomed cake tin. Line the tin with most of the pastry, pressing it up the sides so that it is about 1 cm (½in) higher than the top edge of the tin. Put the remaining pastry aside.

Now, cover the pastry with a thin layer of the breadcrumbs or matzo meal. Spoon the apple mixture into the pastry case and turn the extra pastry in over the filling. Cut the remaining pastry into strips and lay over the top in a lattice pattern. To glaze, brush these with the milk and melted apricot jam. Bake in the pre-heated oven for 1 hour.

Serve hot or cold with fresh whipped cream. This cake also freezes well. To do so, wrap the unbaked cake in cling film, tin as well, and, when it has frozen, remove from the tin and re-wrap. To cook, simply defrost, return to a prepared tin and bake as given above.

GRANDMA DELLA'S APPLE COCOA CAKE AND GRANDMA SUMMERS' RHUBARB CUSTARD PIE

Kimberley Summers O'Brien, Leytonstone, East London

Della Macaluso Owens was born in Coal City, Illinois, in 1904 – the first-born of two Sicilian immigrants. She was a seamstress and married Jack, an Irish immigrant who was a coal miner.

Mae Sapp Summers was also born in 1904 in Bath, Illinois – a small, rural community where Mae's father owned a livery stable. She trained as a teacher and married Clarence, a farmer and a fireman. Mae made marvellous American quilts.

Kimberly Summers O'Brien has fond memories of her two American grandmothers. 'These recipes are both very unusual in Britain, but even in the USA they both stand out as truly delicious,' says Kimberly. 'Both my grandmothers were excellent bakers and cookery teachers. Della would only cook the Apple Cocoa Cake in the autumn, when the apples were at their peak. Rhubarb Pie, however, appeared only in the spring, when Grandma Summers picked fresh rhubarb from the garden. Luckily, my two grandfathers enjoyed gardening and so they could provide their wives with fresh fruit and vegetables. I was always encouraged to help in both camps, acting as picker, carrier and peeler; greasing endless tins and rolling out the dough scraps for my "doll pies".'

GRANDMA DELLA'S APPLE COCOA CAKE

SERVES SIX TO EIGHT

3 eggs
400g (14oz) caster sugar
100g (4oz) margarine
120ml (4fl oz) water
350g (12oz) plain flour
3 tablespoons cocoa powder
1 teaspoon bicarbonate of soda
1 teaspoon ground cinnamon
1 teaspoon allspice
225g (8oz) walnuts, chopped
100g (4oz) plain chocolate chips
2 medium cooking apples, peeled and grated
1 teaspoon vanilla essence

Pre-heat the oven to gas mark 3, 160°C (325°F). Grease and flour a 30-cm (12-in) ring mould.

Beat together the eggs, sugar, margarine and water until fluffy.

Sift together into a separate bowl the flour, cocoa powder, bicarbonate of soda and spices. Gradually add the dry mixture to the creamed mixture and mix well.

Fold in the nuts, chocolate chips, apple and vanilla essence until they are evenly distributed through the mixture. Spoon it into the prepared tin and bake in the pre-heated oven for 60–70 minutes, until it springs back when gently pressed or a skewer inserted into it comes out clean. Cool on a wire rack for 15 minutes before turning the cake out of the tin.

GRANDMA SUMMERS' RHUBARB CUSTARD PIE

SERVES SIX TO EIGHT

3 eggs
350g (12oz) caster sugar
2 tablespoons plain flour
50ml (2fl oz) single cream
¾ teaspoon ground nutmeg
pinch of salt
750g (1½lb) rhubarb sliced
30-cm (12-in) unbaked pie crust

Pre-heat the oven to gas mark 3, 160°C (325°F).

In a large bowl, beat together the eggs, sugar, flour, cream, nutmeg and salt.

Stir in the rhubarb, then pour the mixture into the pie crust. Bake in the pre-heated oven until the filling has set (about 1 hour).

Leave to cool before serving with whipped cream.

MRS CARLTON'S
FAVOURITE PECAN PIE

Nancy Carlton, Bristol, Avon

Lula Carlton was born in 1872 in San Marcos, Texas. When she married, she moved with her new husband to a small town in West Texas – Fort Davis, which, in those days, was a real frontier community. Life was tough for those early pioneers and the women had to work as hard, if not harder, than their menfolk. Lula was no exception. Apart from raising six children, she also ran a boarding house and kept a large orchard.

Much of her long day was spent cooking – for her family and for her guests. This recipe was a favourite of hers and all those who sat at her table. Lula particularly liked it because it took such little time and effort to make, yet produced such spectacular results.

Her granddaughter, Nancy, still makes the pecan pie using the family recipe and says 'It's deliciously rich and reputed never to fail.'

SERVES SIX TO EIGHT

1 × 20-cm (8-inch) uncooked shortcrust pastry case

For the filling
3 eggs
1 tablespoon flour mixed with 175g (6oz) caster sugar
25g (1oz) butter or margarine, melted
½ teaspoon ground nutmeg
150g (5oz) golden syrup
120g (4½oz) pecan nuts
pinch of salt

Pre-heat the oven to gas mark 4, 180°C (350°F).

Beat the eggs well, then add the flour and sugar, then the butter or margarine and nutmeg and, finally, stir in the golden syrup, nuts and salt.

Pour the mixture into the pastry case and bake for about 45 minutes, until the filling has set.

GATEAU AU CHOCOLAT MAMAN

Suzanne Bleakley, Congleton, Cheshire

Jeanne Ach was born into a Jewish family in 1904 in Mulhouse, Alsace, when it was under German occupation. She married a distant cousin, Edmund Ach.

When the Second World War broke out, Edmund went into the Army, but was captured and sent to a prisoner of war camp in Germany. Being Jewish, Jeanne, her three young boys and her parents had to hide from the Nazis – first in the Jura and, then, further west in Limoges. 'This was a terrifying time for my mother who lived in constant fear of being captured and sent to a concentration camp,' says her daughter, Suzanne. Luckily the family all survived the War and were reunited in Selestat, where Suzanne and another brother were born.

Jeanne Ach in 1944.

Suzanne says this recipe is 'A chocolate cake which tastes slightly different each time I make it.' The recipe has been passed down through generations.

SERVES EIGHT

5 eggs, separated
pinch of salt
200g (7oz) dark chocolate
150g (5oz) caster sugar
200g (7oz) ground almonds
2 tablespoons eau de vie or
  brandy

Pre-heat the oven to gas mark 4, 180°C (350°F). Grease a loose-bottomed 23-cm (9-in) cake tin and line the bottom with a circle of greased greaseproof paper.

Whisk the egg whites with the salt until they are quite stiff.

Grind the chocolate, keeping it cold so it does not melt.

Mix the egg yolks and sugar until they are well combined then gradually add the other ingredients in turn – some almonds, then some chocolate, then some egg white – mixing well all the time by hand or you can do this in a blender.

Add the *eau de vie* or brandy.

Pour the cake mixture into the prepared cake tin and bake in the pre-heated oven for 1¼ hours.

113

BAKED FUDGE PUDDING

Deb Goodenough, Newport, Isle of Wight

Fudge pudding is as North American as popcorn and peanuts. This recipe is wicked – a chocoholic's dream.

It comes from Maria Lukaniuk, who was born in 1920 in Belorussia. Her father had been a poor forester but he and his family emigrated with hopes for a better life to Alberta, Canada, when Maria was nine. However, things were no more comfortable there to begin with and the family lived for quite a time in a 'sod house', one made from grass turves.

Maria's mother had had a very hard childhood and continued to struggle after she married. She and Maria's father 'broke' a small farm and her normal day consisted of milking 30 cows, morning and evening, by hand, growing enough vegetables to see her family through the long, hard winter, clothing them and, of course, cooking!

For the rural wives of Alberta, 'farming circles' were one of their main social events. During these they used to chat and swap recipes. This is where Maria was given the recipe that she passed to her daughter, Deb Goodenough.

SERVES SIX

150g (5oz) plain flour, sieved
100g (4oz) caster sugar
2 teaspoons baking powder
¾ teaspoon salt
2 tablespoons cocoa powder
100g (4oz) walnuts, chopped
120ml (4fl oz) milk
1 teaspoon vanilla essence
25g (1oz) butter, melted
50g (2oz) cocoa powder
175g (6oz) soft brown sugar
1 teaspoon vanilla essence
400ml (14fl oz) boiling water

Pre-heat the oven to gas mark 4, 180°C (350°F).

Sift the first five ingredients into a bowl. Then, stir in the nuts, milk, vanilla essence and melted butter. Spread the mixture in a greased square cake tin approximately 20 by 20cm (8 by 8in) and 5cm (2in) deep.

Mix the cocoa powder and brown sugar together and sprinkle this over the pudding batter.

Add the vanilla to the boiling water and pour this over the mixture in the tin, too. Bake for 40–45 minutes.

Serve the pudding hot or warm; it is delicious with vanilla ice-cream.

Above right: The passport photograph of Maria Lukaniuk (centre) and her family when they emigrated to Canada from Russia. Right: Maria as a young woman in Alberta.

WACKY CHOCOLATE CAKE

Nancy Smith, Chertsey, Surrey

This eggless chocolate cake might take a little nerve to make the first time, but it works well even if it is rather 'wacky'. It comes, originally, from British Columbia, Canada, and has been handed down through three generations to Nancy Smith, who came to England in 1971 to train as a nurse.

The recipe originated with her Aunt Helen. Nancy was brought up in French-Canada and only met her once. It took the family an epic journey of three days and four nights to get to British Columbia, which is nearly as far from Montreal as it is from Britain.

One of Nancy's ancestors was a founder of British Columbia. He started life as Mr Smith but obviously found it rather tiresome to have such a commonplace name and decided to change it to something much more memorable – Amour de Cosmos! Perhaps he too enjoyed the Wacky Chocolate Cake.

Nancy remembers her mother making the cake on her baking day. 'In those times you would do things on a certain day and I remember coming home on baking day to these wonderful smells. When I make this cake, I always think of Mum. She was a fabulous sweet cook. I'm the savoury chef. What a wonderful team we would have been.'

During the war people used to use vinegar as a substitute for eggs. Although food shortages may have been a reason for the creation of this cake, that doesn't mean it is austere. It keeps well – for about a week – but it has normally disappeared by then.

SERVES SIX TO EIGHT

225g (8oz) plain flour
200g (7oz) caster sugar
3 tablespoons cocoa powder
1 teaspoon salt
1 teaspoon baking powder
1 teaspoon baking soda
1 tablespoon distilled (white) vinegar
1 teaspoon vanilla essence
40g (1½oz) white vegetable fat, melted
250ml (8fl oz) very hot water
icing sugar or icing of your choice to decorate

Below: Nancy with Aunt Helen, 1962.

Pre-heat the oven to gas mark 4, 180°C (350°F).

Sift the first six ingredients on to a piece of greaseproof paper. Sift again into a 20-cm (8-in) ungreased tin. The remaining preparation of the cake is done in the tin.

Make 3 holes in the flour mixture. In one hole put the vinegar, in the second put the vanilla essence and in the third put the melted vegetable fat. Stir the mixture.

Pour the very hot water over the mixture and mix well with a fork. Bake in the pre-heated oven for 30–45 minutes – until it springs back when lightly pressed in the middle or a skewer inserted in the centre comes out clean. When baked, leave it in the tin to cool completely.

Turn the cake out of the tin and dust with the icing sugar or ice with vanilla-flavoured or other icing of your choice.

THREE AUSTRIAN RECIPES

Polly Zinram, Charlbury, Oxfordshire

Polly Zinram was born into a large Jewish family in Vienna. She remembers a summer house in a small village in Southern Moravia, part of Austria until 1918 but now part of the Czech Republic. These recipes come from the heartland of rich desserts.

Tragically, many of Polly's relatives died in the Holocaust, but she says that 'those of us who remain have brought their much-loved and much-used recipes to England and the USA to hand on to future generations'.

Her grandmother, Josephine Sax, married at 15 and died, already an old woman at 35, giving birth to her twenty-first child.

Five sons and nine daughters survived, 'Grosspapa was renowned for his beautiful and virtuous daughters and wished that all his children had been girls,' recalls Polly.

The motherless children were looked after by Tante Bertha. 'Every morning she would get up first. She would walk down the lane to buy freshly baked crescent-shaped rolls at the tiny bakery. They had poppy seeds on top and could not be matched anywhere,' says Polly. 'I remember, as a child, visiting my aunts, who gave huge weekend parties. They all sat bolt upright around the table and were forever warning me about the slippery slopes

and pitfalls of life – this was very intimidating for a young girl!' Here are three of Polly's favourite recipes.

NUT AND CHOCOLATE CREAM GATEAU

SERVES SIX TO EIGHT

For the cake
4 eggs
150 g (5 oz) caster sugar
90 g (3½ oz) hazelnuts, almonds
    or *walnuts, ground*
90 g (3 ½ oz) plain chocolate,
    finely grated or warmed just
    enough to be pliable

For the fillings
325 ml (11 fl oz) real or
    vegetable whipping cream,
    lightly whipped
225 g (8 oz) raspberries, fresh or
    frozen and defrosted, sieved
sugar, to taste
3 tablespoons drinking chocolate
    powder
1 teaspoon instant coffee powder
    or *granules mixed in a little*
    hot water

First, make the cake. Pre-heat the oven to gas mark 3, 160°C (325°F). Grease and flour three 15-cm (6-in) diameter cake tins.

Place the eggs and sugar in a bowl

Below: Grosspapa and his fourteen surviving children.

and beat until light and fluffy and trebled in volume.

Gently fold in the ground nuts and chocolate.

Pour the mixture into the three prepared tins. Bake in the pre-heated oven for about 12 minutes, or until they are firm to the touch and a skewer inserted into the centre comes out clean. Remove from the tins immediately and leave to cool on wire racks.

Now, make the three different fillings. Take a third of the whipped cream and add the sieved raspberries and sweeten with sugar to taste. Spread on top of the first cake, on a cake plate, to form the bottom layer, and place the second cake on top.

Take half the remaining cream and add the drinking chocolate powder to it, then spread it over the top of the second cake.

Place the third and last cake on top.

Add the coffee to the remaining cream, adding sugar to taste, and pipe this on top of the cake. Keep refrigerated.

FRUIT LOAF

SERVES SIX TO EIGHT

6 eggs, separated
120g (4½oz) caster sugar
1 teaspoon vanilla essence
grated rind of ½ a lemon
1 tablespoon brandy, rum or
*   sherry (optional)*
140g (5oz) self-raising flour
150g (5oz) mixed dried fruit
50g (2oz) raisins

For the sugar syrup
120g (4½oz) caster sugar
150ml (5fl oz) water
1 orange

Pre-heat the oven to gas mark 3, 160°C (325°F). Prepare a 1.5-litre (2½-pint) loaf tin by lining it with greased greaseproof paper or baking parchment.

Place the egg yolks and half the sugar in a bowl and beat until light and fluffy and trebled in volume. Gently fold in the vanilla essence and grated lemon.

In another bowl, whisk the egg whites until they form soft peaks, add half the remaining sugar and continue beating until the egg whites are stiff and shiny. Fold in the remaining sugar and the alcohol, if using.

Add the flour, dried fruit and raisins to the egg yolk mixture and mix well. With a large metal spoon, gently fold in the egg whites.

Pour into the prepared loaf tin and bake in the pre-heated oven for 1 hour, or until a skewer inserted into the centre of the loaf comes out clean.

Meanwhile, make a sugar syrup. Place the sugar and water in a pan and boil rapidly until it reduces, becoming thick and syrupy. Take the peel from the orange, remove all the pith from it and cut into fine, julienne strips. Add these to the hot syrup and pour over the baked cake.

EMPEROR'S SOUFFLE

75g (3oz) plain flour
1 tablespoon sugar
pinch of salt
3 eggs, separated
250ml (8fl oz) milk
120ml (4fl oz) single cream
1 tablespoon oil
25g (1oz) butter
50g (2oz) icing sugar

Make a batter by sifting flour, sugar and salt into a bowl. Make a well in the middle and pour the egg yolks into it. Mix, stirring the egg yolks first, then gradually incorporating the dry ingredients.

Add the milk and cream, whisking well to produce a smooth batter. Beat the egg whites until they are stiff, then gently fold them into the batter.

Heat the oil in a frying pan until it is smoking, then add the butter. Ladle in enough batter to cover the pan. Cook until it is brown and then turn over and brown the other side. Take two forks and tear into medium pieces in the pan and allow to brown appetizingly. Remove from the pan and dredge with sugar. Repeat the process until all batter has been used up. Serve immediately with raspberry syrup or stewed plums.

STUFFED MONKEY

Ruth Edwards, South East London

King's Hall in East London was a famous establishment that catered for many bar mitzvahs, weddings and other Jewish functions. It was run, after the War, by Rebecca Isaacs, who was born and brought up in Warsaw in a family of bakers.

When the Nazi persecution of the Jews began, Rebecca fled to London. There she married into a well-known family of fishmongers from Petticoat Lane, the Rudas. Her Polish baking expertise did not go to waste, however, because she soon started working at King's Hall in nearby Commercial Road.

This recipe has been passed through the generations – to her daughter, Minnie, thence to her granddaughter, Evelyn, and, finally, to Ruth, her great-granddaughter. 'I am sure my Polish relatives would have been astounded to know that this dish would end up in a cookery book.'

SERVES EIGHT

For the pastry
225g (8oz) self-raising flour
175g (6oz) butter
175g (6oz) soft brown sugar

½ teaspoon freshly ground cinnamon stick
1 egg, separated

For the filling
50g (2oz) lemon peel, finely chopped
50g (2oz) ground almonds
40g (1½oz) butter, melted
1 egg yolk

Pre-heat the oven to gas mark 4, 180°C (350°F).

Mix all the pastry ingredients together, except the egg yolk and white. Add the yolk last (reserve the white for later) to form a pliable dough.

Grease a round, 20-cm (8-in) cake tin and line the base with half the mixture. You will need to press it flat with a palette knife as it is too rich to roll.

Mix the filling ingredients together, then spread the mixture evenly over the pastry base. Cover with the other half of the pastry mix. Brush with the reserved egg white, then bake in the pre-heated oven for about 30 minutes or until golden brown. Leave to cool in the tin, then slice into thin pieces – it is very rich!

FRUIT SALAD MOULD

Yvonne Cull, Harlow, Essex

Agnes Stewart was born in Christchurch, New Zealand, in 1901. Her husband managed a timber mill in the West Coast forests of the Southern Alps. Agnes used to cook for the family by the hot stone pit method traditionally used by the Maoris. She also made her own soap and candles and she sewed clothes for her family using a much-prized treadle machine.

During the War, she left her husband. In order to make ends meet, Agnes took a series of jobs as a live-in housekeeper. Yvonne, her daughter, went to 11 schools in 6 years: 'One minute my mother would be catering for the ravenous appetites of sheep-shearing teams and the next the lavish dinner parties of wealthy former employees. Her reputation as a creative and innovative cook spread and she later went on to become housekeeper-chef for society ladies. These women were always trying to outdo one another with the lavishness of their dinner parties and my mother was forever creating new recipes to satisfy their demands. Fruit Salad Mould was first cooked by mother during the last War – it takes me back to the New Zealand summers of my youth.'

SERVES SIX

350 ml (12 fl oz) water
sugar to taste
juice and grated rind of 2 large
    oranges
40g (1½oz) custard powder
2 large cooking apples, peeled
    and grated
2 bananas, sliced
1 × 440-g (1-lb) tin pineapple
    pieces, drained
1 × 425-g (15-oz) tin guavas,
    sliced
6 passion fruit, pulp collected
    from skins
3–4 kiwi fruit, peeled and sliced

Into a large saucepan put the water, sugar and orange juice and rind. Bring to the boil and boil for 5 minutes. Remove the pan from the heat. Mix the custard powder with a little water and add it to the pan, return it to the cooker and gently stir until the mixture thickens, ceasing to be runny.

Remove the pan from the heat and stir in the remaining ingredients, mixing them all together thoroughly and evenly. Spoon the mixture into an attractive large glass or other bowl and refrigerate overnight before serving. Serve with whipped cream.

CINNAMON BALLS

Margaret Davis, Welwyn, Hertfordshire

Evelyn Davis came from a typical close-knit Jewish family of cousins and friends, with whom she spent most of her life. Her father was a publican in the East End of London and Evelyn was born in Whitechapel, just after the First World War. She lived above the pub and learned a lot about cooking.

Her daughter-in-law, Margaret Davis, did not come from a Jewish background, but Evelyn was very warm and welcoming to her. 'The one thing from my husband's culture and religion she specifically handed me was this recipe – deliberately unleavened cakes to produce for visitors during the Passover Festival.' Margaret remembers their first Easter/ Passover as a married couple, when they ate hot cross buns and cinnamon balls together. 'Never having tasted cinnamon balls before, I was very anxious when I first cooked them for my husband's relations. I am not the world's greatest cook, so it was wonderful to be universally praised for my effort by my new relations.' Now the family serves them with Christmas cake.

'The piece of paper my mother-in-law gave me looks rather like a shipwrecked mariner's message that has been at sea many months in a bottle; it is brown, shredded and thoroughly antiquated. It has moved house with us twice and we hope it will stay with us forever.'

What distinguishes this version from the usual cinnamon balls is that they must not be overcooked.

MAKES THIRTY BALLS

2 eggs
225g (8oz) ground almonds
225g (8oz) caster sugar
25g (1oz) ground cinnamon
50g (2oz) fine matzo meal
about 1 tablespoon milk
icing sugar, for dusting

Pre-heat the oven to gas mark 4, 180°C (350°F).

Beat the eggs in a mixing bowl until frothy. Then, mix in all the other ingredients, except the icing sugar.

Roll the dough into balls about the size of ping pong balls and put them on to a greased baking tray. Bake in the pre-heated oven for 5–7 minutes. Take care not to overcook them – they should be dry on the outside and soft inside; all the cooking should accomplish is to change the colour.

Transfer them to wire racks to cool, then roll them in the icing sugar to finish them off.

Right: Evelyn Davis.

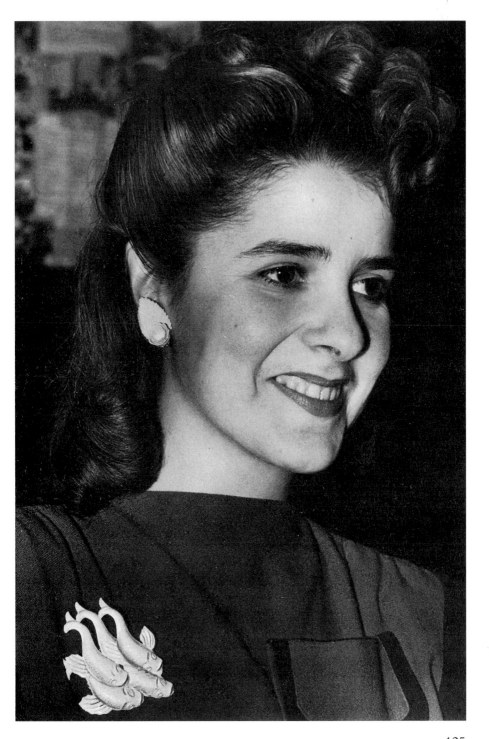

PLONS FREDDO

Edward Urry, Kent

This family favourite is known affectionately as 'roll about sweet'. Why? 'Have some and find out,' says Edward Urry mysteriously. He was passed this recipe by his Italian aunt and it will appeal to those with a sweet tooth. It is also quite unusual.

SERVES FOUR TO SIX

360g (12½oz) butter
330g (11½oz) icing sugar
8 Amaretti biscuits
50g (2oz) plain chocolate, grated
4 eggs, lightly boiled, shelled and finely chopped
200ml (7fl oz) Jamaican rum
8 egg yolks

8 trifle sponges
Maraschino in which to soak the trifle sponges

Mix the butter and icing sugar together thoroughly.

Break up the Amaretti biscuits, then crumble them. Add them, the grated chocolate, the lightly boiled eggs and the rum to the mixture and stir until thoroughly mixed together.

Now, add the egg yolks and beat until the mixture is smooth.

Soak the trifle sponges in the Maraschino until they have absorbed it, then line a large bowl with them. Pour in the sugar and egg mixture, smooth the top and chill in the refrigerator for a day.

INDEX

Alice's Christmas cake 62–3
almond paste 62, 63
apple:
   apple cake Ernst 109
   Aunt Polly's clove and apple
     pudding 42
   German apple torte 107
   Grandma Della's apple cocoa
     cake 110–11
   herring and apple pie 84–5
   mock goose 90
   stirrup 38
   sweet apple chutney 6
asparagus:
   Mum's impossible pie 82
Aubergine Afghani 104
Aunt Louise's cake 52
Aunt Nettie's steak loaf 73
Aunt Polly's clove and apple
   pudding 42
Aunt Winnie's beef roll 74
Auntie's steamed salmon soufflé 86

Baba's polenta 103
bacon:
   cheese and bacon whirls 19
   Mum's impossible pie 82
   Scotch scallops 77
baked beans, barbecued 96
Baked fudge pudding 114
Banana chutney 17
Barbecued baked beans 96
Bate pie 79
beans, haricot:
   barbecued baked beans 96
beef:
   Aunt Nettie's steak loaf 73
   Aunt Winnie's beef roll 74
   olives 97
   tattie bake 80
Bet's bread pud 34
biscuits, Easter 57
brandy sauce 64
bread, milk 54, 56
bread pudding 34
butter cream icing 49

cakes:
   apple cake Ernst 109
   apple cocoa 110–11
   Aunt Louise's 52
   chocolate biscuit 43
   Christmas 62–3
   fruit loaf 120

gateau au chocolat maman 113
   nut and chocolate cream
     gateau 118–19
   old English cider 51
   pepper 46
   ratafia 22–3
   Reeve 49
   shaley 50–1
   sponge 53
   wacky chocolate cake 116–17
   youma loaf 44
Cathrine's party sole 93
cauliflower, Messoda's 105
Chapel toffee 66
cheese:
   and bacon whirls 19
   savoury bread 54, 56
Chicorée d'enfance au gratin 101
chocolate:
   biscuit cake 43
   cream 28–9
   gateau au chocolat maman 113
   Grandma Della's apple cocoa
     cake 110–11
   nut and chocolate cream
     gateau 118–19
   Reeve cake 49
   wacky chocolate cake 116–17
Christmas cake 62–3
Christmas pudding 58–9 see also
   brandy sauce
chutneys:
   banana 17
   sweet apple 6
cider cake 51
Cinnamon balls 124
Clootie dumpling 36–7
clove and apple pudding 42
cocoa see chocolate
coconut:
   Mum's impossible pie 82
cod:
   salt cod with vegetables 95
cream:
   chocolate 28–9
   lemon 22–3
   Swiss 26–7
cream pudding 32
Curried lentil soup 72
custard pie, rhubarb 111

desserts:
   apple stirrup 38
   chocolate cream 28–9

Emperor's trifle 121
   fruit salad mould 123
   German apple torte 107
   lemon cream and ratafia cakes
     22–3
   Plons Freddo 126
   stuffed monkey 122
   Swiss cream 26–7
   see also pies; puddings; tarts
dumplings:
   clootie 36–7
   potato soup and 68

Easter biscuits 57
Emperor's soufflé 121
Estonian spring milk soup 92

False fish 88
fish see cod; herring; salmon; sole;
   tuna
Foaming brandy sauce 64
forcemeat balls 13
fruit:
   Isle of Wight pudding 35
   loaf 120
   salad mould 123
   see also apple; banana; lemon;
    rhubarb
fudge pudding 114

game:
   Mother Maud's Norfolk game
     platter 14–15
   see also hare; rabbit
Gateau au chocolat maman 113
German apple torte 107
glacé icing 42
Grandma Benbow's sticky
   marmalade tart 40
Grandma Della's apple cocoa
   cake 110–11
Grandma Summers' rhubarb
   custard pie 111
Grandma's season pudding 20
Granny Scott's whisky flambé
   clootie dumpling 36–7
Great grandmother Mason's
   cream pudding 32

hare, jugged and forcemeat balls 13
haricot beans:
   barbecued baked beans 96
Herring and apple pie 84–5
hot cross buns 54, 56

127

icing:
butter cream 49
for Christmas cake 63
glacé 42
Isle of Wight pudding 35

Jugged hare and forcemeat balls 13

lamb:
Nanna Crawshaw's neck of
mutton stew 16
special Persian mixed rice 99
leek:
Bate pie 79
lemon:
bomb pudding 21
cream 22–3
tarts 24
lentils:
curried lentil soup 72
false fish 88
soup 70

marmalade tart 40
marrow, pickled 18
meat *see* beef; hare; lamb; rabbit
Messoda's cauliflower 105
milk:
bread 54, 56
Estonian spring milk soup 92
rabbit cooked in 11
mincemeat 60–1
Mock goose 90
Mother Maud's Norfolk game
platter 14–15
Mother's baked rabbit 10
Mrs Carlton's favourite pecan pie
112
Mum's impossible pie 82
mutton stew 16

Nanna Crawshaw's neck of
mutton stew 16
Norfolk game platter 14–15
Nut and chocolate cream gateau
118–19

Old English cider cake 51

pastry:
for apple cake 109
cheese and bacon whirls 19
shaley cakes 50–1
shortcrust 40, 79, 84

Pecan pie 112
Pepper cake 46
Persian mixed rice 99
Pickled marrow 18
pies:
Bate 79
herring and apple 84–5
Mum's impossible 82
pecan 112
rhubarb custard 111
thrift 83
Plons Freddo 126
polenta, Baba's 103
pork sausagemeat:
Grandma's season pudding
20
potatoes:
Bate pie 79
mock goose 90
potato soup and dumplings
68
sausage stovies 76
Scotch scallops 77
tattie bake 80
prawns:
Mum's impossible pie 82
puddings:
baked fudge 114
Bet's bread 34
Christmas 58–9
clove and apple 42
cream 32
Grandma's season 20
Isle of Wight 35
lemon bomb 21
Suffolk pond 39
tipsy 33
Pumpkin au four 100

rabbit:
cooked in milk 11
mother's baked 10
stew 9
Ratafia cakes 22–3
Reeve cake 49
rhubarb:
Grandma Summers' rhubarb
custard pie 111
rice:
false fish 88
special Persian mixed 99
'Robert' sauce 101

salmon soufflé 86

Salt cod with vegetables 95
sauces:
foaming brandy 64
'Robert' 101
Sausage stovies 76
season pudding, Grandma's 20
Scotch scallops 77
Shaley cakes 50–1
shortcrust pastry 40, 79, 84
sole:
Cathrine's party 93
soufflé, steamed salmon 86
soups:
curried lentil 72
Estonian spring milk 92
lentil 70
potato 68
what's intillit 69
Special Persian mixed rice 99
Sponge cake 53
steak loaf, Aunt Nettie's 73
stews:
Nanna Crawshaw's neck of
mutton 16
rabbit 9
Stuffed monkey 122
Suffolk pond pudding 39
Sweet apple chutney 6
Swiss cream 26–7

tarts:
lemon 24
sticky marmalade 40
Tattie bake 80
Thrift pie 83
Tipsy pudding 33
toffee 65
chapel 66
tuna:
Mum's impossible pie 82

vegetables:
Estonian spring milk soup 92
lentil soup 70
salt cod with 95
what's intillit soup 69
see also asparagus; aubergine;
cauliflower; leek; marrow;
potatoes; pumpkin

Wacky chocolate cake 116–17
What's intillit soup 69

Youma loaf 44